The Triad Area

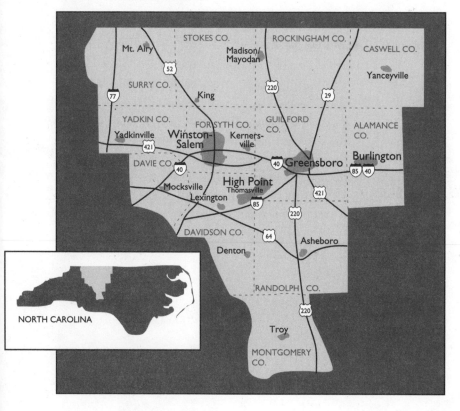

NORTH CAROLINA

Other Trail Books by the Author

Hiking and Backpacking (1979, 1983, 1989, 1994)
North Carolina Hiking Trails (1982, 1988, 1996)
The Trails of Virginia: Hiking the Old Dominion (1984, 1995)
South Carolina Trails (1984, 1989, 1994)
Hiking and Backpacking Basics (1985, 1992)
Hiking the Mountain State: The Trails of West Virginia (1986, 1997)
Monongahela National Forest Hiking Guide (1988, 1993)
Adventuring in Florida, Georgia Sea Islands and Okefenokee Swamp
    (1991, 1995)
Trails of the Triangle (1997)

TRAILS
OF THE
TRIAD

Over 140 Hikes in the Winston-Salem/
Greensboro/ High Point Area

Allen de Hart

John F. Blair, Publisher   Winston-Salem, North Carolina

The paper in this book meets the guidelines
for permanence and durability of the
Committee on Production Guidelines for
Book Longevity of the Council on Library Resources.

Cover photographs (clockwise from left):
Old Salem in Winston-Salem, Guilford Courthouse
National Military Park in Greensboro (both photos
courtesy of North Carolina Travel and Tourism
Division, Raleigh), The Haley House in High Point
(courtesy of High Point Historical Society, Inc.)

Design and composition by Liza Langrall
All photographs by author unless otherwise noted
Printed and bound by R. R. Donnelley and Sons, Inc.

Library of Congress Cataloging-in-Publication Data:

De Hart, Allen.
Trails of the Triad : over 140 hikes in the Winston-Salem /
Greensboro / High Point Area / Allen de Hart
p.   cm.
Includes index.
ISBN 0-89587-161-0 (alk. paper)
1. Hiking—North Carolina—Winston-Salem Metropolitan Area—Guidebooks.
2. Hiking—North Carolina—Greensboro Metropolitan Area—Guidebooks.
3. Hiking—North Carolina—High Point Region—Guidebooks.
4. Trails—North Carolina—Winston-Salem Metropolitan Area—Guidebooks.
5. Trails—North Carolina—Greensboro Metropolitan Area—Guidebooks.
6. Trails—North Carolina—High Point Region—Guidebooks.
7. Winston-Salem Metropolitan Area (N.C.)—Guidebooks. 8. Greensboro Metropolitan
Area (N.C.)—Guidebooks. 9. High Point Region (N.C.)—Guidebooks. I. Title.
GV199.42.N662W554 1997
796.51'09756'6—dc21   96-53451

CONTENTS

Chapter 4   Trails in Municipal Parks and Recreation Areas   63

Chapter 5   Mountains-to-Sea Trail   117

ACKNOWLEDGMENTS

This guidebook is the result of a continuing increase in urban trails and the request of some Piedmont Triad hiking groups that I focus on the trail growth. It was suggested that I select sections of the third edition of *North Carolina Hiking Trails* and make them more user-friendly with maps and photography. Although this meant some duplication of text in the two guidebooks, *Trails of the Triad* fully covers the three major cities of Greensboro, Winston-Salem, and High Point and the surrounding area within a radius of about 50 miles.

The Triad area is dear to me because of my childhood years and my graduation from High Point College (now University) after the Korean War. Born in Patrick County, Virginia, which adjoins Stokes and Surry Counties in North Carolina, I was about five years old when my 17-year-old brother, Moir, took me walking at Hanging Rock and Pilot Mountain. These scenic areas were not state parks then. In those days, the height of excitement for me at Pilot Mountain was climbing a ladder and rock ledges to the top of the knob. Among my other fond childhood memories are the fairs, circuses, theaters, and outdoor farmers' market in Winston-Salem. The tallest building in the city at that time was the R. J. Reynolds Building; riding an elevator for the first time was as much fun as climbing Pilot Mountain.

Assisting me in both the revision of *North Carolina Hiking Trails* and the writing of *Trails of the Triad* were members of the Piedmont Appalachian Trail Hikers (PATH) in Greensboro, an organization I have been a member of since its creation in 1965. Significant support came from Don and Kathy Chatfield in Greensboro. Don's mother, Louise Chatfield, was the principal force in the founding of PATH and the North Carolina Trails Association. Another faithful supporter was Harold White of High Point, my Theta Chi fraternity brother and roommate at High Point College.

Kelly Cagle, forestry technician for Uwharrie National Forest, provided updated information on the Triad's longest trails. In meeting with the staff of the Greensboro Parks and Recreation Department, I received the assistance of Ed Deaton, cultural and historical manager; Jim Sykes, resource manager; and Dan Maxton, manager of Bur-Mill Park. Also helpful was Roger Bardsley, Guilford County planner.

In Winston-Salem, I received assistance from Nick Jamison, director of the city's Recreation and Parks Department, and Judy Hunt, principal planner of the City-County Planning Board of Forsyth County and Winston-Salem. In High Point, I received assistance from Michael Ingram, recreation supervisor of the Parks and Recreation Department, and Dick Thomas, executive director of Piedmont Environmental Center.

Other assistance came from Janice McDonald of the Greensboro Area Chamber of Commerce, Judy Mendenhall of the High Point Chamber of Commerce, and Andrea Logan of the Greater Winston-Salem Chamber of Commerce. I am also grateful for the assistance of those who provided shuttle transportation, arranged logistics, and participated in trail measurements. They were Linda McKiddy, Benjamin Luques, Tony Butler, Daren Matthews, Ray Matthews, Jason Lake, Lee Jones, Travis Combest, Wendy Michel, Jason Mason, Laurie Cullen, Michael Piazza, and Russell Tarlton.

I received photographic assistance from the North Carolina Department of Travel and Tourism, the Winston-Salem Office of Parks and Recreation, and the Photofinishing Services Division of the Touchberry Group in Raleigh.

Gordon Hardy, publisher of Appalachian Mountain Club Books in Boston, and Carolyn Sakowski (president) and Steve Kirk (editor) of John F. Blair, Publisher, in Winston-Salem deserve special thanks for arranging and exchanging my research material to make *Trails of the Triad* possible.

INTRODUCTION

The Piedmont Triad has a population of about 1.2 million in 12 counties. In Guilford County are the cities of Greensboro (population 200,000) and High Point (73,000). Winston-Salem (179,000) is in Forsyth County. The other counties considered part of the Triad are Alamance, Caswell, Davie, Davidson, Montgomery, Randolph, Rockingham, Stokes, Surry, and Yadkin. Geographically, Greensboro, High Point, and Winston-Salem are near the heart of North Carolina and are central to the state's commercial crescent, which stretches from Raleigh to Charlotte. Although the three major cities are in the rolling hills of the Piedmont, it is less than an hour's drive to mountain terrain at Hanging Rock State Park and Pilot Mountain State Park to the north. In addition, it is about 50 miles northwest from Winston-Salem to the scenic Blue Ridge Parkway, or southeast to the wilderness of Uwharrie National Forest. From Greensboro, it is about 30 miles south to the outstanding North Carolina Zoological Park. In addition to these and other attractions, visitors find the Triad's weather ideal. The average annual temperature is about 68 degrees, the rainfall about 50 inches, and the snowfall about 3.8 inches.

The term *Piedmont Triad* originated in 1986, when executive directors of the chambers of commerce in Greensboro, High Point, and Winston-Salem discussed the high cost of long-distance telephone calls among the three cities. Following the formation of the Piedmont Triad Chambers Group, a dialogue among the chambers, the telephone companies, and the North Carolina Utilities Commission lasted six years before a successful regional plan was completed. During the process, the chambers had the airport renamed Piedmont Triad International Airport in

1987, created a postmark for the Piedmont Triad in 1990, and designed "Piedmont Triad Community" city-limit signage to identify local towns.

In recent years—particularly from 1994 to 1996—the Triad has been listed in the nation's top 10 areas for attracting new industry, according to *Site Selection and Industrial Development*. In 1994, *Entrepreneur* magazine named the Triad "one of the best cities for small business." The *National Business Employment Weekly*, published by the *Wall Street Journal*, has ranked the Triad fifth among American metropolitan areas for beginning a career. The Triad excels in its outstanding quality of life. It has seen recent growth in industry, banking, medicine, historic preservation, higher education (the area is home to 22 colleges and universities), the arts, sports, and parks and recreation. It is the latter on which this book will focus.

The historic city of Winston-Salem had its origins in 1753 when Moravians—considered the oldest international Protestant denomination—established a settlement known as Bethabara. The settlers named another tract of land Salem in 1766. In 1849, the state legislature formed Forsyth County and named the town of Winston—only 1 mile from Salem—the county seat. The "Twin City" was consolidated in 1913. If the city could have a third name, it might be Reynolds. One of Winston-Salem's original downtown skyscrapers still carries the name of industrialist R. J. Reynolds, and his family's historic mansion is Reynolda House on Reynolda Road.

In 1995, Winston-Salem was one of three cities in the world recognized for successful downtown economic development by the International and Downtown Association. The city is also recognized for its continued development in the arts. Here is housed the North Carolina School of the Arts, the first professional residential school of its kind in the nation. The concept of local arts councils was developed in the city, and its council is one of only 22 in the nation to raise more than $1 million annually.

This city of art also boasts the Southeastern Center for Contemporary Art, Reynolda House Museum of American Art, the Moravian Music Foundation, and at least nine other visual-arts organizations and galleries. In addition, there are more than 14 choral, theater, and music centers and organizations. The city can perhaps trace its cultural heritage to Moravian artistic expression.

Winston-Salem is also known for its health centers—North Carolina Baptist Hospital/Bowman Gray School of Medicine among them—and its expansive parks and recreation system, which offers a range of greenways, recreational facilities, and trails.

High Point is widely known for its International Home Furnishings Market, attended by furniture representatives from every state in the nation and 85 foreign countries. The city is also home to the Furniture Discovery Center, the only museum in the United States centered around furniture design, and the Furniture Library, which holds the world's largest collection of literature on the history of furniture. High Point received its name from being the highest point on the railroad between Goldsboro and Charlotte.

Greensboro was named after Revolutionary War hero Nathanael Greene; it was initially called "Greensborough" or "the Town of Greene." Nicknamed the "Gate City" because of its early and easy access to railway travel, the city is now a hub for two interstates, three major federal highways, and an international airport. The area's largest city, it boasts the Greensboro Coliseum complex, one of the largest in the state. The city is also home to the six-week Eastern Music Festival, which features professional and student musicians from around the world. *U.S. News and World Report* recently listed Greensboro 20th among 100 top cities in the nation for housing values, and the *New York Times* has included the University of North Carolina at Greensboro among its "Best Buys in College Education." The National Science Foundation has recognized North Carolina Agricultural and Technical State University as the largest producer of African-American engineers in the nation.

Greensboro has 3,000 acres of parkland; there is some type of park within 1 mile of each city resident. In Forsyth County, the 1,300-acre Tanglewood Park, located a few miles west of Winston-Salem, offers recreation for all seasons. In High Point are Piedmont Environmental Center and a long section of *Bicentennial Greenway Trail*, a trail that will connect High Point and Greensboro.

This book not only describes foot trails for day hikes in the Triad's metropolitan areas, but foot trails within a 50-mile radius as well; it thus includes a few counties not officially part of the Triad. Published information on the Triad is available from the major cities' chambers of commerce in cooperation with the Piedmont Triad Chambers Group. The Greensboro Area Chamber of Commerce may be contacted at 910-275-8675; the number for the Greater Winston-Salem Chamber of Commerce is 910-725-2361; the number for the High Point Chamber of Commerce is 910-889-8151. Among the publications helpful for residents, visitors, and newcomers are *North Carolina's Piedmont Profile* (published in Greensboro by *Business Life Magazine*), *Piedmont Triad Newcomer* (published annually in Raleigh by Bond Publishing, Inc.), *Triad Business News* (published weekly by the *High Point Enterprise*), and the *City Guide* for Winston-Salem (published annually by the *Winston-Salem Journal*).

Variety of Trails

There are over 140 trails in the Triad and the surrounding region that offer easy access for users. The longest trail for hiking, backpacking, and camping is the 20.5-mile *Uwharrie Trail* in Uwharrie National Forest south of Greensboro; if using the connecting *Dutchmans Creek Trail*, another 11.1 miles may be added. Among the shortest trails are a cluster of botanical paths at the Natural Science Center in Greensboro and *Fence Row Trail* at Piedmont Environmental Center in High Point. Multiple-use greenway systems exist in all three major cities; Winston-Salem's *Strollway Trail* is nearest to a downtown area.

Examples of greenways for walkers, the physically impaired, joggers, bikers, and in-line skaters are *Boulding Branch Trail* in High Point, *Silas Creek Trail* in Winston-Salem, and *Barber Park Trail* in Greensboro. Among the interpretive trails are *Chestnut Oak Nature Trail* at Hanging Rock State Park and *Emerson's Walk* at Tanglewood Park. A special trail with Braille is *Bicentennial Garden Trail* in Greensboro.

For equestrians, there are horse trails at Pilot Mountain State Park, Uwharrie National Forest, and Cedarock Park in Alamance County. *Sauratown Trail*, an equestrian trail on private land, is being relocated for a connection between Hanging Rock State Park and Pilot Mountain State Park. (Call the Sauratown Trail Association at 910-368-2673 for an update on construction.)

Mountain-bike routes are located in Uwharrie National Forest and in some municipal areas (see map page 15); *Bald Eagle Trail* at Lake Higgins northwest of the Greensboro city limits is an example. Street bicycling is allowed on almost all the municipal greenways. Two of the state's longest bicycle trails pass through the Triad. The Department of Transportation's *Mountains-to-Sea Bike Route* #2, from Murphy to Manteo, passes through Yadkin, Forsyth, Davidson, Guilford, and Alamance Counties. *North Line Trace Bike Route* #4, from Mouth of Wilson, Virginia, to Currituck, North Carolina, passes through Surry, Stokes, Rockingham, and Caswell Counties.

For canoeists, there is *Yadkin River Trail*, which flows through the counties of Surry, Yadkin, Forsyth, Davie, and Davidson.

See chapter 5 for information on the *Mountains-to-Sea* foot trail corridor.

Maps

Although the maps in this guidebook may prove helpful, it is essential that you have a state and a city map if you are unfamiliar with the area. Free state maps are available at interstate welcome centers, chambers of commerce, some state and city park offices, and the Highway Map Office (Department of Transportation, 1 South Wilmington Street, Raleigh, NC 27601, 919-733-7600). Available for purchase at bookstores and most convenience stores is Delorme's detailed *North Carolina Atlas and Gazetteer*. County maps may be helpful for rural areas; these are sold by the Highway Map Office, chambers of commerce, and county register of deeds offices. Thomas Publications' *North Carolina County Maps* contains maps of all the state's counties in atlas form and is sold in some bookstores.

Health and Pleasure

Walking is our most natural exercise, a historical, biological, and cultural asset. Henry David Thoreau, considered one of America's greatest walkers, said he walked for both health and pleasure. Walking for exercise and mental strength was also part of the philosophy of such people as John Ruskin, William Wordsworth, Jane Austen, Thomas Jefferson, Abraham Lincoln, Harry Truman, Emma Gatewood, and coast-to-coast Robert Sweetgall. A more recent figure of note is Warren Doyle, who in 1995 completed the *Appalachian Trail* for the 10th time, a world record.

Walking magazine reported in a 1995 survey of "Why Americans Walk" that 80 percent walk to enjoy the natural scenery, 75 percent for exercise and health, 40 percent for errands, and 17 percent for commuting to work or school. For urbanites, even a walk on the sidewalk is good for health and pleasure. Sidewalks can provide a nature walk for viewing birds, squirrels, flowers, trees, streams, and lakes. In some cities, there are historic districts where sidewalks and nature paths are combined.

The networking of greenways, a product of the 1980s, is enhancing walking options.

Health specialists say that simple exposure to sunlight on a sidewalk or nature trail can assist in beating the wintertime blues and cabin fever. Health therapist Paula Alder claims that we can "walk out" our problems. A walking habit helps in staying active, shaving off calories, and "dealing more positively with issues." On urban greenways, walkers are likely to see pedestrians walking fast, running, or jogging to lose weight. In 1991, the Weight Control Information Network reported that 31 percent of American adults were overweight, a 10 percent increase from 1962. Despite the benefits of modern medicine, we cannot abandon our need for a healthy diet and plenty of exercise. The most natural and inexpensive method for beginning to acquire and maintain physical and mental health is to take a walk every day. One of the purposes of this book is to emphasize how close you are to walks on alluring and inspiring nature trails in the Triad area.

Planning Your Nature Walks

Who Is Going?

Judgments of where to go and what to take can usually be made quickly by experienced hikers. Beginners may need some assistance from experienced hikers, sports specialists, scoutmasters, or outdoor sports coaches. Outdoor sports associated with walking include backpacking, camping, canoeing, and fishing; the latter may require a license. Some parks offer fields for baseball, football, and soccer, courts for basketball and tennis, and beaches for swimming. With such a variety of options available, you will need to plan what gear you will take and what size vehicle you will need. Even with the use of this book, you may need additional maps or have additional questions about the services or schedules at the parks. It is likely that the parks will have brochures or signs to assist in your decisions after your arrival.

For parents taking their children on trails and picnic outings, part of the planning may involve choosing a park with a playground or a nature museum. If taking senior citizens or those who need wheelchairs, check appendix 2 for suggested trail choices. This book also identifies parks that offer boat, bike, or horse rentals. A few parks have nature tour guides.

Are Your Feet Ready?

A vital part of your plans for walking or hiking should be to have proper footwear. A study made by the American Podiatric Medical Association in 1996 revealed that about 62 percent of Americans assume that it is normal for their feet to hurt, and that about 80 percent endure some type of foot pain regularly. Yet hardly 3 percent visit a podiatrist to determine the cause. A large percentage of people buy shoes from salespeople who are not trained in recommending the best shoes for their customers. A frequent comment is that after you "break them in," shoes will be comfortable. If the shoes are of poor quality, do not have proper toe-box space or arch support, or are in need of custom foot beds and cushioning, you are likely to have discomfort or damage your feet. When replacing good shoes, take the pair with you to a qualified salesperson to assist in the choice of your new shoes. Usually, one foot is larger than the other. The thickness of socks is also an important factor in proper fitting.

If you are a walker, runner, and backpacker, you will need different shoes for each activity. Walking shoes do not need as much heel cushion as running shoes. For most walkers, the heel buildup of running shoes can cause shin muscles to be strained or pulled. When buying backpacking boots, you may wish to examine the "Gear Guide" edition of *Backpacker* magazine or discuss your wishes with a specialist at an outdoor supply store. Dave Getchell, equipment editor of *Backpacker*, says buying hiking boots is like a search for love. In either search, impulsiveness can cause trouble, but a careful match can form a bond for many years. When being fitted for your shoes, ask the salesperson to use a Brannock measuring device.

For foot maintenance, wear two pairs of socks (one wool or synthetic and one lightweight liner acrylic); wear ankle-high gaiters to prevent skin erosion; protect sore spots with moleskin; wash and dry your feet daily on long trips (there are about a quarter-million pores in the sweat glands); and use foot powder occasionally.

Where in the Triad will you need hiking boots? Among other places, in Uwharrie National Forest; in Hanging Rock, Morrow Mountain, and Pilot Mountain State Parks; on the Greensboro watershed trails; and on *Salem Lake Trail*.

Trail Clothes

Colin Fletcher wrote in *The Complete Walker III* that the best trail clothes are none at all. In his long hike through the Grand Canyon, he lived by that principle, wearing only boots to protect him against rattlesnakes and a big hat for shade. With all respect to one of America's most authoritative writers on walking, his fashions are not appropriate for the Triad trails. Instead, hikers should first consult the weather forecast and wear what is comfortable. Walkers can settle the most serious matter of dress when they pamper their feet with perfect shoes. Clothes should keep you warm and dry, in thermal equilibrium. If it is cool and you are sweating due to fast walking, jogging, or running, you may need both an absorbent garment and a Gore-Tex shell. Whatever you choose, be aware of the risk of hypothermia when cooling down too rapidly.

Long-sleeve shirts and trousers are recommended for brushy trails in such places as Uwharrie National Forest, the state parks, and the lake trails, where ticks and other biting bugs can easily get on your skin. Some experts also recommend light-colored clothing. If you are hiking on game lands or hunting preserves during hunting season, you must wear an orange-blazed jacket and cap. If backpacking on long or overnight trails in the Triad, choose extra clothing appropriate for the season. Local trail-supply stores have an outstanding diversity of trail clothes and gear and can provide counsel on what is best for your excursions.

What's in Your Daypack?

A daypack (waist or shoulders) is desirable when you will be on a trail long enough to need water, food, rainwear, or first aid. Some trail consultants insist that you should take a daypack if you are going to be out of sight of your home or vehicle. Among the basics items you will need are maps, water, nutritional food, a first-aid kit, a pocketknife, insect repellant, a flashlight, a whistle or other alarm, a handkerchief, spare clothing, a rain jacket with a hood, notepaper, and pens. You should also carry FastAid, a small, folding, cardlike first-aid guide that provides instructions for dealing with 31 potential emergencies; there is a place on the guide to include emergency telephone numbers for ambulance, rescue squad, personal doctor, hospital, and family members. If you are on a nature outing, you may need a camera and binoculars. How often have you caught yourself saying, "If only I'd taken my camera"? Children—particularly those between the ages of nine and 15—usually like to be outdoors regardless of whether they are hiking, playing games, or exploring. They will enjoy the trails even more if accompanied by siblings or friends in the same age group. Make a daypack for each of them. And finally, if the family dog is large enough, provide it with a "dogpack" for its food and water.

Trail Security

The trails in this book are unlighted, with the exception of a few short trails in town or city parks. They do not have designated police patrols except at most parking areas in urban locations during the night. Do not expect emergency telephones. The first rule of security is not to hike after dark. Many of the signs at the trailheads specifically state that the trails are closed after dusk. Other security suggestions are to lock your vehicle and to not leave valuable items where they can be seen through the windows; to inform someone in your family or a friend where you are going and when you expect to return; to always keep your eyes and ears alert (headsets with loud music may interfere with the sounds of impending danger); to take a cellular telephone with you; and, of course, to have one or more partners with you whenever possible.

Walking on a wide, scenic greenway, seeing so many happy faces, hearing laughter from children playing, and sharing friendly greetings with strangers may make you wonder how anything could go wrong. But it has in the past and will again. If you are concerned about the safety of a trail, call the park office or the city police. If you notice any threat to trail safety, it may prove helpful to other hikers if you report the incident quickly.

Trail Courtesy

Some trail courtesy rules are distinctive to a locality, some are written on signs in parks and subdivision greenways, and others are generally accepted but unwritten. On multiuse trails, the first rule is to share space, much as on sidewalks and streets; on some multiuse trails, bikers are encouraged to use a bell or gentle horn to alert pedestrians of their approach. Pedestrians have the right of way unless posted otherwise. Signs indicating that some trails are for foot travel only should be respected. Pets must be kept on a leash and prevented from soiling treadways and playgrounds. Avoid leaving trash on the trails, damaging

plants, harassing wildlife, and playing boom boxes at offending vol-
umes.

How friendly you are to strangers depends on your personality and
the reasons for the conversation. Taking photos or serving as a tour
guide is an automatic icebreaker. A neighborhood walker and fitness-
trail user on *Salem Creek Trail* once told me of his experience with neighbors upstream who always passed him without greetings. That is, until
one morning when an unleashed dog chased a frightened kitten up a
trailside tree. Participants in the successful rescue not only greet each
other now, but sometimes stop for conversations as well.

Welcome to the trails of the Triad.

LEGEND FOR MAPS

Hiking Trail

Bicycling, Equestrian, or General

Railroad

Parking Lot

Information

Telephone

Picnic Table

Picnic Shelter

Restroom

Camping

Fishing

Swimming

Shower

Wheelchair Accessible

TRAILS OF THE TRIAD

Backpackers on the Uwharrie Trail, Uwharrie National Forest

Chapter 1

TRAILS ON UNITED STATES GOVERNMENT PROPERTIES

Of the variety of national parks, monuments, historic sites, and battle-fields in North Carolina, only one—Guilford Courthouse National Military Park—is located in the Triad.

The area is also home to Uwharrie National Forest, the smallest of the four national forests in the state. North Carolina is the birthplace of professional forestry management in the United States. In 1892, George Vanderbilt employed Gifford Pinchot to manage Vanderbilt Forest at Biltmore in Asheville. Pinchot's success prompted Vanderbilt to purchase an additional 120,000 acres, a section of which later became part of Pisgah National Forest. In 1895, renowned German forester Carl Schenck succeeded Pinchot. Pinchot was later influential in the establishment of the United States Forest Service; Schenck went on to found the first forestry school in America. Nantahala and Croatan National Forests are the other national forests in the state.

W. Kerr Scott Dam and Reservoir, located on the Yadkin River, is one of the four major United States Army Corps of Engineers projects in North Carolina. All were constructed for the purpose of preventing downstream flood damage. The Corps leases acreage to the state's Wildlife Resources Commission for wildlife management and motor-boat registration in all four projects. Formed during the early years of the nation as part of the Continental Army, the Corps had its beginning at West Point, a garrison on the Hudson River. In 1798, the Corps was enlarged, and in 1802 Congress made West Point a military academy. Since then, Congress has authorized a wide range of Corps projects: blazing and building roads, clearing waterways and harbors, building dams, protecting and restoring shorelines, providing disaster relief, ensuring fish and wildlife development, and enhancing recreational opportunities.

GUILFORD COURTHOUSE NATIONAL MILITARY PARK
Guilford County

This park was established March 2, 1917, in honor of the 4,300 officers and soldiers of General Nathanael Greene's Continental Army in the battle against British field commander Lord Charles Cornwallis on March 15, 1781. Although the battle was not a total victory for either side, it was significant in that Cornwallis retreated to Wilmington and practically abandoned the Carolinas. The end of the Revolutionary War came seven months later at Yorktown, Virginia.

The 220.4-acre park has a museum in its visitor center and seven tour stops of historical interest. Camping is not allowed. The park is open daily except Christmas Day and New Year's Day.

Address and Access: Superintendent, Guilford Courthouse National Military Park, 2332 New Garden Road, Greensboro, NC 27410 (910-288-1776). An access to the park is from the junction of Wendover Avenue and Westover Terrace (US-220). Go northwest 3.9 miles on Westover Terrace to New Garden Road. Turn right (east) and go 0.5 mile.

Guilford Courthouse Battlefield Trail

Length and Difficulty: 2.5 miles, easy

Trailhead and Description: From the visitor center, follow the paved trail southwest of the parking area through a mature forest of oak, hickory, walnut, and poplar with an understory of dogwood, redbud, and sourwood. The first tour stop—the American first line—is at 0.4 mile. You

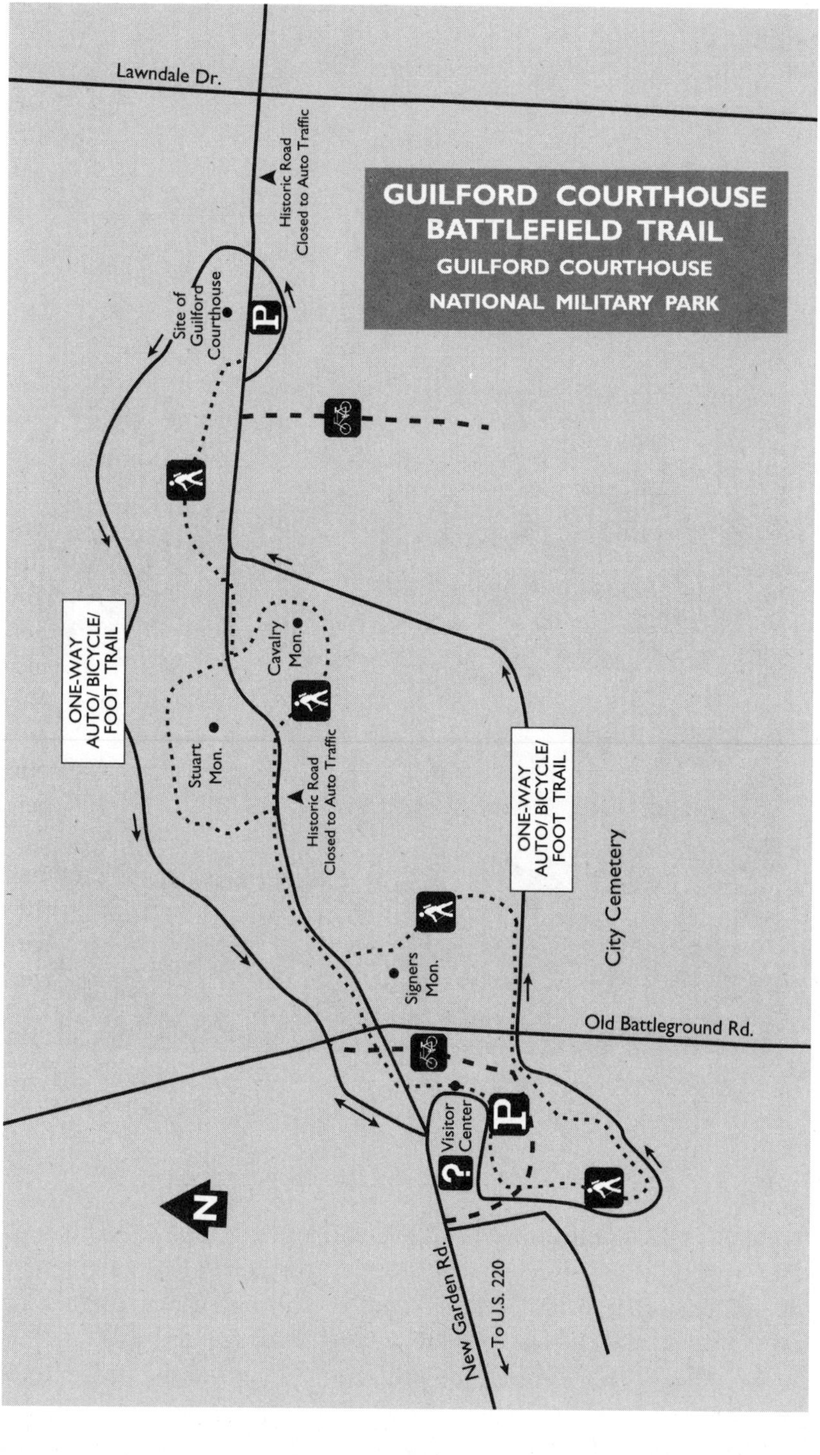

GUILFORD COURTHOUSE
BATTLEFIELD TRAIL
GUILFORD COURTHOUSE
NATIONAL MILITARY PARK

Lawndale Dr.

Historic Road
Closed to Auto Traffic

Site of Guilford Courthouse

P

ONE-WAY AUTO/BICYCLE/ FOOT TRAIL

Cavalry Mon.

Stuart Mon.

Historic Road
Closed to Auto Traffic

ONE-WAY AUTO/BICYCLE/ FOOT TRAIL

City Cemetery

Signers Mon.

Old Battleground Rd.

Visitor Center

P

N

New Garden Rd.

To U.S. 220

Guilford Courthouse Battlefield Trail

will cross Old Battleground Road and reach a spur trail leading left to the General Greene monument at 0.6 mile. Continue on the trail through open fields of large, scattered oak and poplar with senna, milkweed, evening primrose, lobelia, and bur marigold among the wildflowers. At 1.3 miles, you will reach the fifth tour stop at the site of Guilford

Courthouse. (From the parking area on the right, walking a few yards west on the road leads to a 0.2-mile walking/biking trail into Greensboro's Country Park. See chapter 4 for information on trails in this park.) You will reach the sixth stop—the American third line—at 1.9 miles and return to the visitor center at 2.5 miles.

UWHARRIE NATIONAL FOREST

In the center of the state, the 49,000-acre Uwharrie National Forest spreads into a patchwork of private and public tracts in three counties. The forest is mainly in Montgomery County, but more than 8,000 acres are in Randolph and another 1,000 acres in Davidson. Nearly 300 miles of county, state, and private roads form part of that patchwork, and another 185 miles of forest roads give easy access to the forest's streams, recreational areas, and trails.

The origin of the name *Uwharrie* is unclear; perhaps it came from the Suala Indians. As early as 1701, it was spelled *Heighwaree*; a map of 1733 lists it as *Uharie*; and it is listed as *Voharee* on a 1770 map. With its mountainous range rarely over 900 feet in elevation, the forest disguises its 400-million-year history. Archaeologists have reported that the composite geography has been eroded by the Yadkin, Pee Dee, and Uwharrie Rivers to expose parts of the hard basalt and rhyolite deposits in the oldest known mountain range in North America. Its rocky and worn ridges have been mined for gold, silver, copper, and lead, and early settlers impoverished an already poor soil with inadequate timber and farm management.

In 1931, much of the acreage was identified as the Uwharrie Purchase Unit, and in 1935 it was transferred to the United States Forest Service for administration. Finally, in 1961, it became a national forest. During the 1930s, the Civilian Conservation Corps and subsequently the United States Forest Service reforested hundreds of acres with pine and allowed groves of hardwoods to mature in the coves and by the stream banks. Slopes with mountain laurel, dogwood, and sourwood became natural understory gardens featuring 700 species of plants and abundant wildflowers and ferns. A further preservation was made in 1984 when federal Public Law 98-324 created the 4,790-acre Birkhead Wilderness Area. The "Final Environmental Impact Statement" of the

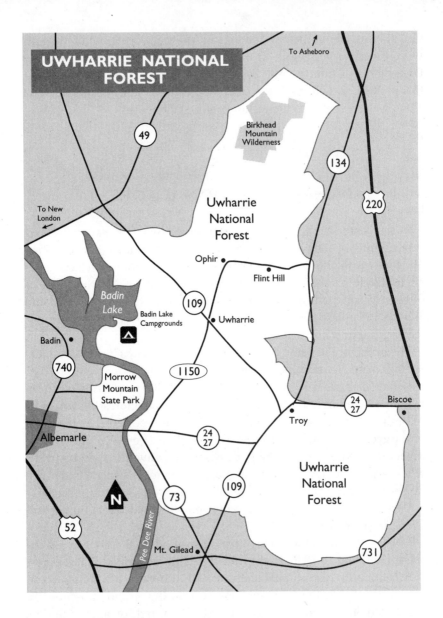

To Asheboro

Birkhead
Mountain
Wilderness

49

134

220

To New
London

Uwharrie
National
Forest

Ophir •

• Flint Hill

Badin
Lake

Badin Lake
Campgrounds

109

• Uwharrie

Badin •

740

Morrow
Mountain
State Park

1150

Albemarle

24
27

24
27

Biscoe

•

Troy •

N

73

109

Uwharrie
National
Forest

52

Pee Dee River

Mt. Gilead •

731

1986 Land and Resource Management Plan recommended 255 historic
sites "for further testing or preservation."

The recreational facilities include three family campgrounds. Uwharrie
Hunt Camp has tent sites with picnic tables, drinking water, and sanitary facilities. To access this campground from the intersection of NC-
109 and SR-1150 at the community of Uwharrie, drive 1.5 miles north

on NC-109 to a sharp left on SR-1153. Follow SR-1153 for 0.4 mile; the hunt camp is on the right. The new Arrowhead Campground (completed in 1996) has 50 tent sites, 35 of which have individual electrical hookups, picnic tables, and drinking water. A bathhouse, flush toilets, and a waste-disposal system are also offered. To access this campground from Uwharrie Hunt Camp, follow FR-576 off SR-1153 for 2.9 miles to FR-597. Turn right, then take the first left on FR-597B. The old Badin Lake Campground has tent sites, picnic tables, drinking water, and toilet facilities. Access is the same as for the new campground, except travel farther on FR-597 to FR-597A, on the left. Another campground, Badin Lake Group Camp, has a large field for tent camping; it also offers drinking water and toilet facilities. Reservations are required for the group camp. Access is on the same road leading to the old Badin Lake Campground, but turn right near the campground entrance. There is a fee for all the campgrounds except Uwharrie Hunt Camp. All of the campgrounds are open year-round. They offer boat launching to Badin Lake at Cove Boat Ramp, accessible at the end of FR-597B, described above. A new boat ramp is planned at the old Badin Lake Campground; it already has a floating fishing pier. The lake has largemouth bass, white bass, bream, yellow perch, sunfish, and catfish.

There are two primitive camps in the national forest. West Morris Mountain Camp offers picnic tables and vault toilets. To access this camp from Uwharrie, drive 0.3 mile north on NC-109 from its junction with SR-1150. Turn right on Ophir Road (SR-1303), then go 1.2 miles; the camp is on the right. Yates Place Camp is at the end of a 0.5-mile spur trail leading east off *Uwharrie Trail* 0.1 mile south of the junction of Mountain Road (SR-1146) and FR-6746.

The forest has horse trails on back-country roads, foot trails (the longest of which is the 20.5-mile *Uwharrie Trail*), and 20 miles of ORV trails. The latter are confined to an area between Badin Lake on the west and the Uwharrie River on the east and are accessible south off FR-576. Some of these trails are a 2.1-mile section of *Dutch John Trail* (USFS #90), the 2.8-mile *Rocky Mountain Loop Trail* (USFS #92), the 1.2-mile *Gold Mine Trail* (USFS #93), and the 3.4-mile *Dickey Bell Trail* (USFS #96A). A map is available from the district office.

An interpretive double-loop white-blazed trail, the 0.9-mile or 2.2-mile *Densons Creek Nature Trail* (USFS #97) begins at the ranger station parking lot. Numbered posts describe flora, fauna, history, and geology. Scattered pines are among the hardwoods. The predominant rock formations are milky quartz. The 0.4-mile *Uwharrie Fitness Trail* (USFS

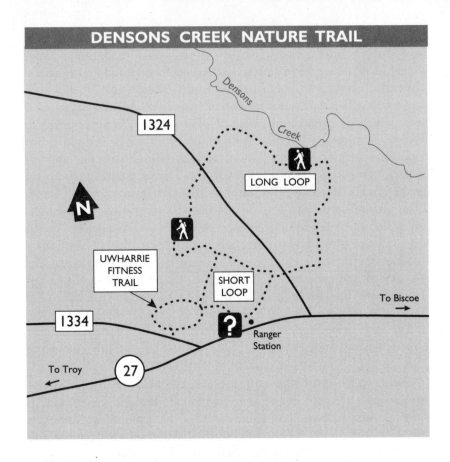

#397) connects with *Densons Creek Nature Trail*, but its parking lot is accessed on the first right turn (Page Road) off NC-24/27 about 0.1 mile west of the ranger station. Maps and brochures are available from the ranger station.

In season, hunting and fishing are allowed in the forest in accordance with state laws and licenses. Forest game animals are deer, turkey, raccoon, squirrel, fox, rabbit, and quail. Numerous species of songbirds, owl, and hawk are here also. Among the species of reptiles are box turtle, lizards, and snakes, including the infrequently seen copperhead.

Address and Access: District Ranger, Uwharrie National Forest, USFS, Route 3, Box 470, Troy, NC 27371 (910-576-6391). Access is on NC-24/27 about 1.8 miles east of Troy.

Support Facilities: Motels, restaurants, and shopping centers are in Troy, Asheboro, and Albemarle, and hospitals are in the latter two. A store for groceries and outdoor sports equipment is at Uwharrie at the junction of NC-109 and SR-1303/1150.

Badin Lake Area
Montgomery County

This is a concentrated recreational area with facilities for boating, fishing, camping, picnicking, and hiking, as described above. At the new Badin Lake Campground, there are asphalt roads, parking spaces, water, electricity, a bathhouse/restroom building, and a sewage-disposal system. If using the former route or the new route to connect with *Badin Lake Trail*, described below, campers have a long loop trail to connect with the other campgrounds. A new boat ramp is planned near the old Badin Lake Campground.

Access: From the junction of NC-109 and Checking Station Road (SR-1153) 1.5 miles northwest of Uwharrie, go 0.4 mile on SR-1153 and turn right on FR-567 at the Uwharrie Hunting Camp/Picnic Area. Drive 2.9 miles and turn right on FR-597. The first left (onto FR-597B) leads 0.5 mile to the new Badin Lake Campground; another 0.5 mile leads to Narrows Reservoir, a picnic area, and Cove Boat Ramp. The second left (onto FR-597A) goes to the old campground and Badin Lake Group Camp.

Badin Lake Trail (USFS #94)

Length and Difficulty: 6.5 miles, moderate

Trailhead and Description: This trail has diamond-shaped white plastic blazes. Because of a lack of maintenance, hikers should pay alert attention to its route.

Begin the trail at the Cove Boat Ramp parking area (described above) and go north along the Badin Lake shoreline. Curve around a knoll on whose top is the new Badin Lake Campground; you will junction with the return loop route on the right at 0.2 mile. (The new campground facilities may change this connection.) Continue ahead by the lake. At 0.5 mile, you will arrive in a rocky cove with ferns and wildflowers. You will enter another cove with white alder, oak, and pine at 1 mile; the old Badin Lake Campground is up the hill. Stay close to the water-

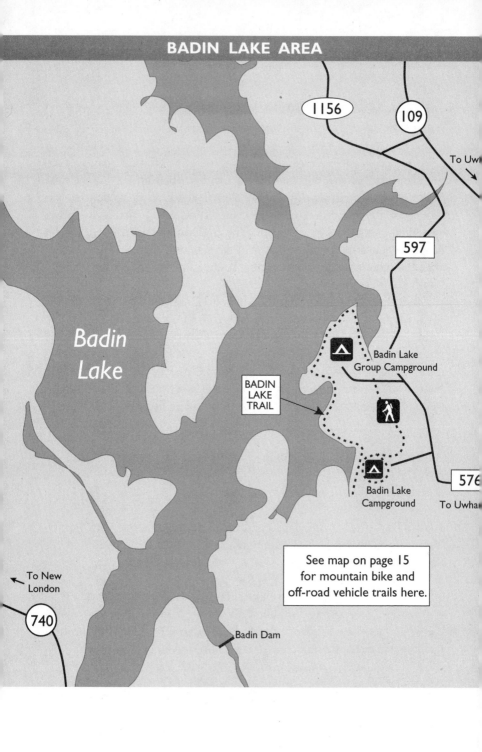

BADIN LAKE AREA

1156

109

To Uwi

597

Badin Lake

BADIN LAKE TRAIL

Badin Lake Group Campground

Badin Lake Campground

576

To Uwha

See map on page 15 for mountain bike and off-road vehicle trails here.

To New London

740

Badin Dam

Badin Lake Trail

front and continue around the campground to a cove at 1.8 miles. From this point, there is less evidence of the campground spur trails. At 2.3 miles, you will enter a cove where the trail leaves the shore and slightly ascends to an old road (right and left) at 2.5 miles. (To the right, the old road goes to Badin Lake Group Camp and FR-597A. To the left, it extends 0.5 mile to the tip of the peninsula.) Ahead are a beautiful, open forest and the other side of the peninsula.

Descend slightly to the lake's edge and pass right of a floating fishing pier. Follow the shoreline to a cove at 2.8 miles, ascend, and curve left to cross a long ravine at 3.2 miles. At 3.3 miles, you will reach a large, sloping rock on the hillside into the lake. Here are lichens, mosses, wildflowers, scrub pine, and laurel. The trail soon ascends on the hillside, then drops to the lake before entering a long and dense cove, a favorite place for spring peeper and bullfrog. At 4.2 miles, you will reach a junction and a sign indicating an access to *Dutch John Trail* ahead. Turn right and proceed steeply to the hilltop at 4.3 miles at the northeast corner of the Badin Lake Group Camp field.

If continuing on *Badin Lake Trail* from the sign, descend to the stream and a rocky area. You will then ascend a ridge, descend, cross a hollow, ascend, and cross FR-597A at 0.7 mile. You will arrive at a wildlife field at 0.8 mile and curve right. You will cross a woods road at 1 mile, pass through a damp area among saplings at 1.1 miles, then cross an old road with patches of wild quinine (*Parthenium integrifolium*) and rabbit's pea. You will cross another road, then descend into more saplings. The trail forks at 1.5 miles before a wildlife field. To the left is a faint 0.1-mile trail to FR-597 a few yards north of its junction with FR-597B. To the right, the trail goes around the wildlife field and enters the new Badin Lake Campground at 1.6 miles. Here, it junctions with the 0.8-mile asphalt bike/hike loop trail that circles the camping area. Hikers should veer slightly right on the asphalt trail to a white oak tree with a white blaze. (The former *Badin Lake Trail* went 0.3 mile through the campground; campers may notice the old white blazes on trees between campsites #2 and #44B.) After passing one of the trail's exits (left), you will arrive at a support wall (right) and red-orange boulders unearthed from the campground construction at 2 miles. A few yards farther, you will see the old diamond-shaped white plastic blazes to the right. Turn right and descend to follow the blazes. At 2.1 miles, you will return to the *Badin Lake Trail* loop at the lakeside. Turn left to return to the restroom and parking lot of Narrows Reservoir, the picnic area, and Cove Boat Ramp, for a total of 6.6 miles. (If there is no official trail route to the lake by the time of this book's publication, it is likely that some campers will have made an unofficial route.) On the exit road, it is 0.5 mile up the hill to the new Badin Lake Campground and another 0.5 mile to FR-597. (USGS-FS map: Badin)

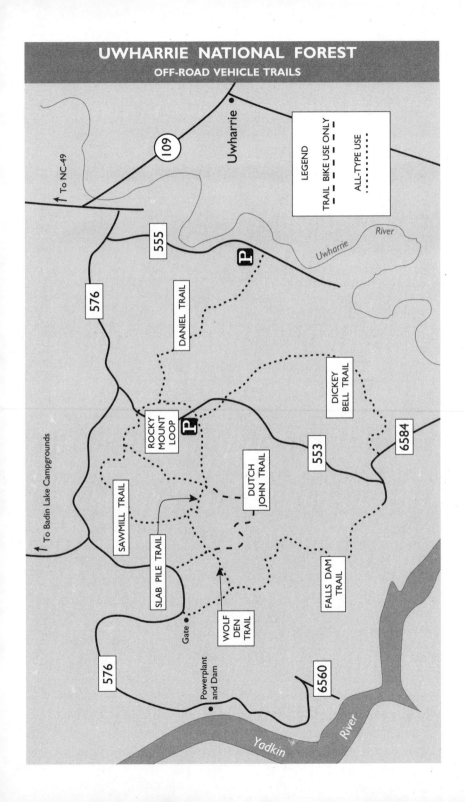

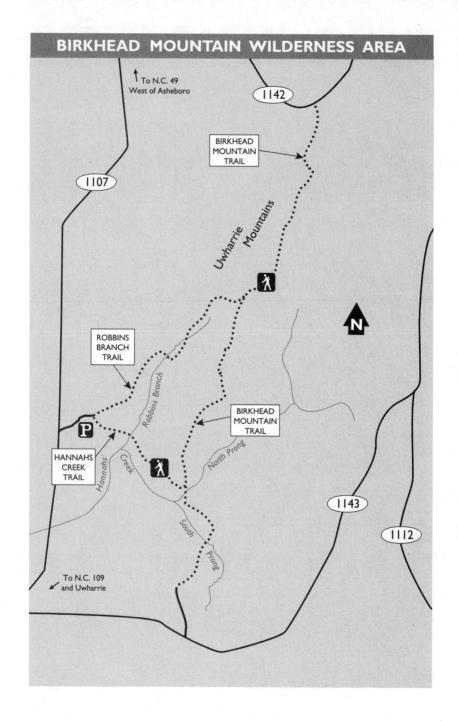

BIRKHEAD MOUNTAIN WILDERNESS AREA

To N.C. 49
West of Asheboro

1142

BIRKHEAD
MOUNTAIN
TRAIL

1107

Uwharrie Mountains

N

ROBBINS
BRANCH
TRAIL

Robbins Branch

BIRKHEAD
MOUNTAIN
TRAIL

North Prong

P

HANNAHS
CREEK
TRAIL

Hannahs Creek

South Prong

1143

1112

To N.C. 109
and Uwharrie

Birkhead Mountain Wilderness Area
Randolph County

Access: From the junction of US-220 and NC-49 in Asheboro, go west on NC-49 for 5.5 miles and turn right on Science Hill Road (SR-1163). After 0.4 mile, turn left (south) on Lassiter Mill Road (SR-1107) and go 5.2 miles to a wilderness sign at FR-6532. Turn left and drive 0.5 mile to the parking area at the end of the road. If arriving from the southwest on NC-49 (11 miles northeast of the NC-109 junction), turn right on Mechanic Road (SR-1170). After 0.7 mile, you will reach the junction with Lassiter Mill Road. Turn right and go 4.3 miles to the wilderness. If traveling from the south, take SR-1303 for 5.3 miles north to Ophir, then follow SR-1134 and SR-1105 for 2.7 miles north to Eleazer, then follow SR-1107 for 5.1 miles north to FR-6532, on the right.

Robbins Branch Trail *(3.2 miles)*
Birkhead Mountain Trail *(USFS #100, 5.6 miles)*
Hannahs Creek Trail *(1.4 miles)*

Length and Difficulty: 10.2 miles combined, easy to moderate

Special Features: pioneer history

Trailheads and Description: These trails do not receive maintenance; some old white blazes remain. Follow the trail sign. At 0.4 mile, you will reach a fork where *Robbins Branch Trail* goes left and *Hannahs Creek Trail* goes right. If following *Robbins Branch Trail*, you will proceed through a young forest and ascend gently. At 1.2 miles, you will pass through an open area of sumac and wildflowers with a vista of the Uwharrie Mountains. You will descend gradually, enter an older forest at 1.5 miles, and pass right of rock erosion barriers left by pioneer farmers at 1.7 miles. Turn sharply left on a footpath at 1.9 miles. After about 90 yards, you will cross Robbins Branch, which is bordered with Christmas fern. Continue upstream to cross the branch three times and a tributary once. In late August, cardinal flower is brilliant near the branch. You will leave the branch's headwaters and junction with *Birkhead Mountain Trail* at 3.2 miles.

To the left, *Birkhead Mountain Trail* goes 2.6 miles to the northern terminus of Tot Hill Farm Road (SR-1142). To the right, it runs 2 miles to a junction with *Hannahs Creek Trail* and another 1 mile to its southern terminus at the forest boundary. If taking the northern route, you will curve right at 0.2 mile to a shallow saddle for a traverse on the crest of Coolers Knob Mountain. You will pass camp #1-B (left) at 0.7 mile, then reach Coolers Knob, with its scenic view east on a 50-yard spur, at 1.4 miles; Cedar Rock Mountain and peaks ranging from 900 to 1,050 feet in elevation are visible from here. You will then descend. At 1.5 miles, you will leave Birkhead Mountain Wilderness Area and cross private land for 0.2 mile before reentering the national forest. You will cross Talbotts Creek at 2.4 miles and reach SR-1142 at 7.2 miles. (To the left, it is 2 miles to NC-49; a right turn on NC-49 leads 5.1 miles to Asheboro.) If taking *Birkhead Mountain Trail* to the right (south), you will pass patches of wild quinine and camp #5 (which offers a grill) at 0.4 mile. You will descend gradually in a hardwood forest and reach the remnants of Birkhead Plantation at 1 mile. Boy Scout Troop 570 has erected a sign about John W. Birkhead (1858–1933), his wife, Lois Kerns (1868–1943), and their 10 children; the family later moved to Asheboro, where John W. Birkhead was clerk of court and county sheriff. At 1.7 miles, you will pass camp #4, located to the right on a spur. At 2 miles is the site of the plantation of Christopher Bingham, which dates from around 1780, and a junction to the right with *Hannahs Creek Trail*. Ahead, *Birkhead Mountain Trail* goes another 0.4 mile to cross the North Prong of Hannahs Creek before reaching a campsite at 0.9 mile. At 1 mile, it arrives at the southern boundary of Birkhead Mountain Wilderness Area and the trail's southern terminus. Ahead, it is 1 mile on a private jeep road to a crossing of the South Prong of Hannahs Creek and SR-1109 at Strieby Church. From there, it is 0.6 mile on the road to a junction with SR-1143. To the right (west), it is 2.1 miles to the Lassiter Mill crossroads with SR-1107; to the left (east), it is 10.8 miles to Ulah and US-220.

On *Hannahs Creek Trail*, follow the old woods road. You will cross a streamlet and pass a chimney and foundation on the left at 0.2 mile. You will cross another streamlet at 0.5 mile, pass a man-made rock wall, and cross Robbins Branch at 0.9 mile. Ascend to the junction with *Robbins Branch Trail* at 1.4 miles. Veer left and return to the parking area. (USGS-FS maps: Eleazer, Farmer)

Uwharrie Trail Area
Montgomery County

Uwharrie Trail (USFS #276)

Length and Difficulty: 20.5 miles, moderate

Connecting Trails: West Morris Mountain Trail (USFS #95, 2.2 miles, moderate); *Dutchman's Creek Trail*

Special Features: Dennis Mountain, Island Creek

Trailhead and Description: Uwharrie Trail, a national recreation trail since 1980, is a north/south route. At its southern end, it forms a reversed S, crosses the middle of *Dutchman's Creek Trail,* and forms an irregular figure eight. Access to the southern trailhead is at a parking lot on NC-24/27 about 2 miles east of the Pee Dee River bridge and 10 miles west of the center of Troy.

From the northwest corner of the parking space, you will enter a footpath through small oak trees and descend on the white-blazed trail into a more mature forest of hardwoods, pine, and laurel. You will pass under a power line at 0.3 mile. At 1 mile, you will cross Wood Run Creek in a laurel grove and at 2 miles junction with a 0.3-mile spur (right) to the Wood Run primitive campsite. At 2.4 miles, you will pass a spur leading a few yards right to FR-517. Follow the trail downstream; you will cross the stream six times. You will observe crested dwarf iris and pass the remnants of an old automobile at 2.5 miles. You will then cross a timber road at 3.5 miles and ascend steeply to the top of Dennis Mountain (732 feet in elevation) at 3.7 miles; there are views of Morrow Mountain State Park and Lake Tillery to the west. Descend, join an old woods road to the right, rock-hop Island Creek at 4.6 miles, turn right on a footpath, and go upstream in a scenic forest featuring galax and royal fern. After crossing the creek four times, you will ascend to and cross FR-517 at 5.6 miles. After about 120 yards, you will arrive at a cross-trail with the yellow-blazed *Dutchman's Creek Trail.* (To the left, or north, *Dutchman's Creek Trail* goes 5.3 miles to rejoin *Uwharrie Trail.* To the right, or south, it goes 5.9 miles to the NC-24/27 parking area. A loop can be formed here for either trail.) Continue on *Uwharrie Trail.* After about 90

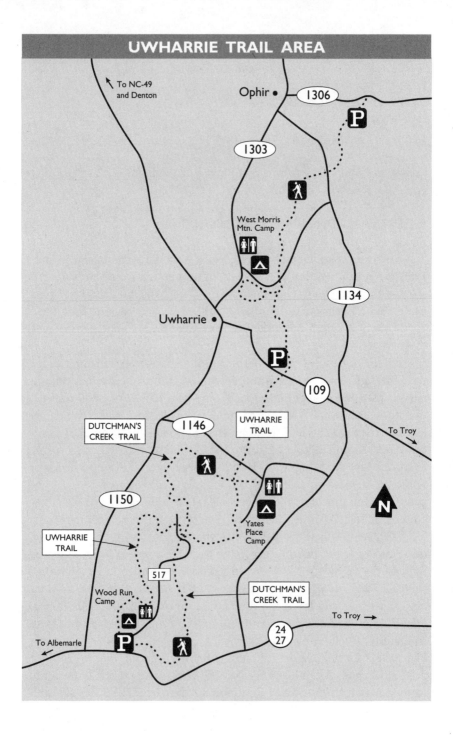

yards, you will cross an old, lightly used forest road. About 275 yards farther along the path, you will arrive at *Pond Camp Trail*, to the right. (This is a 0.3-mile spur trail to a campsite and a small pond at the head-waters of Clarks Creek.) For the next 2.2 miles, the trail ascends and descends three hilltops and crosses three old forest roads and four streamlets before reaching Dutchman's Creek at 7 miles. Deer and tur-key may be seen in this area. The forest is open in a number of places, but laurel is dense near some of the stream areas. At 8.2 miles, you will ascend from a young forest; you will reach a junction with *Dutchman's Creek Trail* to the left at 8.4 miles. At 8.9 miles, you will reach a junction (right) with a 0.4-mile spur trail leading to primitive Yates Place Camp and a good parking area on Mountain Road (SR-1146). At 9 miles, you will arrive at Mountain Road, where the trail crosses. (To the left, it is 2.1 miles to SR-1150. To the right, it is 0.4 mile to Yates Place Camp and then 5 miles on Carrol Road—SR-1147—and NC-109 to Troy.)

Continue ahead on *Uwharrie Trail*. You will cross a tributary of Cedar Creek at 9.3 miles and Watery Branch at 10 miles. Head downstream (right) for 0.5 mile. You will begin a steep, rocky climb and reach the hill summit at 10.8 miles. You will then make a sharp turn off a logging road at 11.3 miles and reach NC-109 at 11.9 miles. Cross the road to a parking space. (To the left, it is 1.8 miles on NC-109 to a junction with SR-1150 and Uwharrie, where groceries, telephones, gasoline, and sup-plies are available. To the right, it is 5 miles to Troy.)

At 12.4 miles is a spring, to the left. You will cross Cattail Creek at 12.8 miles and the Spencer Creek hiking bridge at 14 miles. You will ascend and pass a bed of running cedar at 14.1 miles and intersect with the unblazed *West Morris Mountain Trail* (left) at 14.3 miles. (*West Morris Mountain Trail* descends 1 mile to West Morris Campground, a primi-tive camp on Ophir Road—SR-1303—about 1.2 miles north of Uwharrie; the camp offers tables, grills, and two vault toilets.) On *Uwharrie Trail*, you will ascend and reach the mountain summit at 14.6 miles. You will then cross an old forest road at 15 miles and cross two streams on bridges a few feet apart at Panther Branch at 17 miles. You will cross SR-1134 at 18.1 miles. You will reach a high ridge at 19.2 miles and continue to a rocky peak of Dark Mountain (953 feet in elevation) at 19.4 miles. Here is an excellent western view. After a rocky descent, you will reach a parking area on Flint Hill Road (SR-1306) at 20.5 miles.

Ophir is 1.8 miles to the left, Flint Hill is 2.8 miles to the right, and it is 7 miles to NC-134. The 5.4-mile *Uwharrie Trail Extension* (USFS #99) from here to SR-1143 has been discontinued because of its traverse on private property. (USGS-FS maps: Lovejoy, Morrow Mountain, Troy)

Dutchman's Creek Trail (USFS #98)

Length and Difficulty: 11.1 miles, moderate to strenuous

Connecting Trail: Uwharrie Trail
Special Features: reforestation, old mines, remoteness, Dutchmans Creek

Trailhead and Description: The **S**-shaped *Dutchman's Creek Trail* begins at, ends at, and crosses the middle of the southern section of *Uwharrie Trail*, with which it jointly forms the shape of an erratic figure eight. The trailheads are at a parking lot on NC-24/27 about 2 miles east of the Pee Dee River bridge and 10 miles west of the center of Troy.

The yellow-blazed trail begins at the northeast corner of the parking lot, across FR-517. You will cross a natural-gas line at 0.3 mile, then enter a clear-cut at 0.4 mile and leave it at 1 mile. You will cross a small branch at 1.1 miles and Dumas Creek at 2.2 miles, then ascend steeply to an open area for southern views. At 2.5 miles, turn sharply left (north) at a 1978 reforestation project. You will leave the clear-cut, dip into a ravine, and cross a road to the private Piedmont Sportsmen Club at 3 miles. You will then pass under a power line at 3.1 miles, ascend gently to the top of a long, flat ridge at 4.4 miles, and descend to cross FR-517 at 4.9 miles. You will cross Island Creek twice, then ascend. You will cross FR-517 again at 5.5 miles to ascend a rocky ridge before reaching a level area and a cross-trail junction with *Uwharrie Trail* at 5.9 miles. (On *Uwharrie Trail*, it is 5.7 miles left to NC-24/27 and 3.3 miles right to NC-1146. See the description below.) Follow *Dutchman's Creek Trail* a few yards to cross a lightly used, old timber road and enter a young forest growing from a former timber clear-cut. You will reach a rocky hill at 6.3 miles. Descend into a grove of laurel and follow Little Island Creek for four crossings before ascending steeply on a rocky, scenic mountain of hardwoods, Virginia pine, and wildflowers at 7.3 miles; in the winter, you can see Badin Dam to the west through the trees. You will reach the mountain summit at 7.6 miles, then descend for the next 0.4 mile; notice the disturbed earth from old mines. You will cross a streamlet three times before climbing another steep mountain and reaching the top at 8.6 miles; the Badin Lake area is visible through the trees in the winter, and Lick Mountain can be seen to the east. At 9.1 miles, you will descend to a gardenlike area of laurel, galax, trailing arbutus, and wild ginger (*Hexastylis shuttleworthii*). At 9.5 miles, you will rock-hop Dutchmans Creek and go upstream in a scenic area of gentle cascades and clear pools. You will pass through a mature forest of tall oak, beech, and poplar with scattered holly. You will rock-hop the creek three times before reaching a road at 10.8 miles. Continue straight ahead to reach a junction with *Uwharrie Trail* at 11.1 miles. To the left, it is 0.6 mile on *Uwharrie Trail* to SR-1146. To the right, it is 2.7 miles to rejoin *Dutchman's Creek Trail*.

Volunteer assistance for trail maintenance on both *Uwharrie Trail* and *Dutchman's Creek Trail* is provided by the Sierra Club's Central Piedmont Group from Charlotte and the Uwharrie Trail Club from Asheboro. (USGS-FS map: Morrow Mountain)

W. KERR SCOTT DAM AND RESERVOIR
Wilkes County

This project was constructed by the Corps of Engineers from 1960 to 1962 and named in honor of former United States senator and North Carolina governor W. Kerr Scott (1896–1958). It offers 16 recreational areas, one of which has been leased to Wilkes County and another to a commercial establishment. The lake contains 1,470 acres and is surrounded by 2,284 land acres. Popular aquatic sports are boating, waterskiing, swimming, and fishing. Small-game hunting is allowed at selected areas. Land activities include camping (Bandits Roost Park and Warrior Creek Park have electrical and water hookups and hot showers), picnicking, and hiking. At the manager's office is a 0.3-mile self-guided loop, *Scott Dam Nature Trail*. It has 27 interpretive points for local trees, flowering shrubs, and ferns. Access is described below. Another short trail is the 0.8-mile *Bandits Roost Trail*. It goes from the boat-ramp parking lot of Bandits Roost Campground in area B along the shoreline to a terminus between campsites #25 and #26 in area A. Access is 1.9 miles west on NC-268 from the dam entrance. A longer trail is described below.

Address and Access: Resource Manager, W. Kerr Scott Dam and Reservoir, P.O. Box 182, Wilkesboro, NC 28697 (910-921-3390). The entrance road to the manager's office is on NC-268 about 3 miles southwest of the US-421 junction in Wilkesboro.

Overmountain Victory Trail

Length and Difficulty: 2.7 miles, easy

Trailhead and Description: Now a national historic trail, this was formerly called *Warrior Creek Trail*. Warrior Creek is historically significant because its mouth at the Yadkin River (now under water) was where the Overmountain Men of the Wilkes County militia crossed the Yadkin on September 28, 1780. The army of 350 men continued to Lenoir, where it joined the main patriot army from the mountains of North Carolina, Tennessee, and Virginia. Their march to the historic Battle of Kings Mountain in South Carolina, where Colonel Patrick Ferguson was killed and his Tory army defeated on October 7, 1780, was a turning point in the Revolutionary War. To commemorate this route, the Corps and local citizens' groups have established this trail.

From the NC-268 entrance to the dam, continue southwest 4.3 miles on NC-268 to section F, Warrior Creek Park, and turn right. Go 0.6 mile and turn left at the campground sign. If the campground is open—usually May 1 to September 30—ask for a campground and trail map and drive the 1 mile to the trailhead, following the signs. If the campground is closed, park outside the gate and walk to the trailhead.

From the trailhead parking lot, descend the steps on a well-graded and well-maintained trail. You will pass through a forest of white pine, holly, and tall hardwoods. Galax, yellow root, ferns, and fetterbush decorate the trail and the stream banks. You will cross two footbridges and arrive at the area C camping road at 0.5 mile. Cross the road; you will pass through area E camping at 0.6 mile, then pass a natural spring at 1.1 miles and a picnic area at 1.3 miles. You will then descend into a lush cove on the lake and arrive at an abandoned picnic area at 2 miles. Ahead, you will follow an old woods road and ascend to an abandoned parking area at 2.5 miles. Turn left and follow the road to a Corps gate at 2.7 miles. To the left are a parking overlook and a picnic shelter with scenic views of the lake. To the right, it is 1.3 miles on the paved campground road to the eastern trailhead and the point of origin. (USGS map: Boomer)

Hanging Rock State Park

Chapter 2

TRAILS IN NORTH CAROLINA STATE PARKS, FORESTS, AND HISTORIC SITES

━━━━━━━━━━━━━━━━

The Department of Environment, Health, and Natural Resources (DEHNR) has seven Natural Resources divisions: Aquariums, Forest Resources, Marine Fisheries, Museum of Natural Sciences, Parks and Recreation, Soil and Water Conservation, and Zoological Park. The current administrative form was created in 1989, but a number of reorganizations preceded the change. For example, in 1955, the North Carolina legislature transferred all the state historic sites from Parks and Recreation to a new Department of Archives and History. In 1977, the legislature combined a number of agencies under the Department of Natural Resources and Community Development (DNRCD), which included the Division of Parks and Recreation.

The state parks system is divided into six units of management: state parks, lakes, recreation areas, rivers, trails, and natural areas. All trails in the parks in the Triad area are covered in this chapter.

Interest in the state's natural resources began in the late 19th century. An example is the establishment of a state Geological Survey in 1891 to determine North Carolina's mineral and forest resources. In 1905, the legislature reorganized the survey to create the North Carolina Geological and Economic Survey. When the legislature and Governor Locke Craig learned in 1914 that timber harvesting and forest fires were destroying such valuable areas as Mount Mitchell, the governor, a strong conservationist, went to the area for a personal inspection. The result was a bill passed in 1915 to create the state's first park, with a cost not to exceed $20,000. The management of Mount Mitchell State Park became the responsibility of the Geological and Economic Survey.

In 1925, the legislature expanded responsibility to fire prevention, reforestation, and maintenance of the state parks and forests when the Geological and Economic Survey was phased into the new Department of Conservation and Development. Acquisition was slow; only three of the Bladen Lakes areas were added to the list in the 1920s. But in the 1930s, federal assistance programs became available, particularly the Civilian Conservation Corps (CCC). Between 1935 and 1943, the state acquired six new parks, among them Morrow Mountain and Hanging Rock in the Triad area. The congressional Recreation Area Study Act of 1936 became the blueprint for state parks systems, but the North Carolina legislature appropriated only sporadic funds. From 1945 to 1961, only Mount Jefferson was acquired.

Five state parks and a natural area were added in the 1960s. There was a notable increase in the 1970s, with 11 new parks, eight new natural areas, and the first state recreation area (SRA) at Kerr Lake. This decade of growth came under the administrations of Governors Bob Scott and James E. Holshouser. Within a three-year period, the parklands nearly doubled thanks to the addition of 50,000 acres. Other advances during this period were the beginning of the state zoo, a trust fund for the natural areas, and the State Trails System Act of 1973, which created a master plan for implementing a statewide network of multiuse trails for hikers, bicyclists, equestrians, canoeists, and ORV users, as well as a seven-member citizens' Trail Committee to advise the director of Parks and Recreation.

During the 1980s, three SRAs and one state park were opened. Legislative appropriations were increased but continued to be inadequate for maintenance and land acquisition. The *Winston-Salem Journal* editorialized in May 1987 that "North Carolina has a large financial investment and a priceless natural heritage in its parks. . . . It needs a master plan to overcome a starvation diet." The same month, the legislature passed the State Parks Act, led by Senator Henson P. Barnes. The act established a master plan that "firmly defines the purpose of state parks and requires sound strategy in managing the system."

For many years, North Carolina has been at the bottom of national rankings for funding of park construction, staffing, and maintenance. Voters responded to this neglect on November 2, 1994, when they passed a $35 million bond referendum for a Parks and Recreation Trust Fund and Natural Heritage Trust Fund. It was a first in the agency's history and the largest single appropriation since its creation in 1915. Sixty-five percent of the recreation fund goes to state parks, 30 percent to matching funds for local park projects, and 5 percent to beach access. Phil McKnelly, the division's director, stated that trail supporters were among the many groups who made citizens aware of park system needs.

Among North Carolina's 29 parks, 23 have trails; the parks' 115 trails offer a total of 212.3 miles of hiking. With the exception of western parks that may close temporarily if there are unusually heavy snowstorms, all the parks are open all year. Most parks open daily at 8 A.M. They generally close at 6 P.M. November through February; at 7 P.M. in March and October; at 8 P.M. in April, May, and September; and at 9 P.M. June through August.

Rules are posted conspicuously in the parks. Alcohol, illegal drugs, and firearms are prohibited. Fishing is allowed, but a state license is necessary. Camping facilities (including those for primitive and youth-group camping) for individual parks in the Triad are described in this chapter. When visiting a park, first go to the park office and request a brochure and maps to make your stay a pleasurable and educational experience.

For information on North Carolina's state parks, contact the Division of Parks and Recreation, P.O. Box 27687 (512 North Salisbury Street), Raleigh, NC 27611 (919-733-7275). For information on trails, contact the state Trails Coordinator, Division of Parks and Recreation, 12700 Bayleaf Church Road, Raleigh, NC 27614 (919-846-9991).

The Division of Forest Resources (another division of the DEHNR) administers five educational state forests. One of them, Rendezvous Mountain Educational State Forest, is in the Triad. The locations of the forests are diverse, but their purpose and facilities are generally the same. For example, they all have interpretive displays and trails, primitive walk-in campsites, and picnic areas. They serve as outdoor-living and environmental centers that teachers and other group leaders use as classrooms. Arrangements can be made with each ranger station for ranger-conducted programs. Campsites are free but require permits. Open season for most of the forests is March 15 to November 30; all are closed Mondays and Tuesdays.

There are 23 state historic sites, administered by the Historic Sites Section, Division of Archives and History, Department of Cultural Resources. The sites offer visitor centers with artifacts, exhibits, and multimedia programs about such historic places as the Duke Homestead, Historic Halifax, and the Thomas Wolfe Memorial. The majority of the sites do not have admission charges. Fort Dobbs State Historic Site, located in the Triad, has a walking trail and is described in this chapter. For more information on North Carolina's state historic sites, contact the Department of Cultural Resources, Raleigh, NC 27601 (919-733-7862).

Seven of the parks, forests, and historic sites in the Triad area are covered here. Although the majority of trails in this chapter are short, they are important walks for educational and cultural purposes.

BOONE'S CAVE STATE PARK
Davidson County

This park consists of 110 acres of hardwoods: beech, oak, poplar, elm, and hornbeam. Laurel, rhododendron, wild hydrangea, and wild pink are among the flowering plants. Located on the east side of the Yadkin River and generally undeveloped, the park offers picnicking, fishing, hiking, and a canoe rest stop on the 165-mile *Yadkin River Trail*. (For information on *Yadkin River Trail*, contact the Yadkin River Trail Association, Inc., 280 South Liberty Street, Winston-Salem, NC 27101, 910-722-9346.)

Daniel Boone's Cave Trail is an easy 0.5-mile route. From the parking lot, you will descend 100 yards on a gravel trail with steps to Boone's Cave, on the right. Local legend says that Daniel Boone hid from the Indians here, or that he discovered and explored the 80-foot cave—thus the park's name. (Cave explorers should be prepared to crawl and have dependable flashlights.) Follow the elevated boardwalks to the riverbank access before following a footpath (left) toward a reconstructed cabin built on the site of a structure that may have belonged to the Boone family; according to legend, the family moved here in 1752, when Daniel was 18. Return to the parking lot on the service road to complete the loop. (USGS map: Churchland)

Address and Access: Morrow Mountain State Park, 49104 Morrow Mountain Road, Albemarle, NC 28001 (704-982-4402). From the junction of I-85 and NC-150 halfway between Lexington and Salisbury, go 5 miles north on NC-150 to Churchland. Turn left on Boone's Cave Road (SR-1162) and go 3.8 miles to the parking area.

DUKE POWER STATE PARK

Iredell County

This park is located on the northern shore of Lake Norman, the largest man-made lake in the state, with its 32,510 acres and 520-mile shoreline. Duke Power State Park has 1,458 acres (mostly donated by Duke Power Company) set aside for swimming, boating, fishing, picnicking, camping, and hiking. Norwood Creek and Hicks Creek transect the park. A 33-site campground is open March 15 to November 30; the campground has no hookups but offers hot showers, flush toilets, tables, grills, and a sanitary dumping station. The park harbors more than 800 species of plants. The forest is mainly hardwoods and Virginia and loblolly pine. A subcanopy of sweet gum, dogwood, and sourwood tops numerous ferns and wildflowers. Among the waterfowl are green-winged teal, blue heron, wood duck, and osprey. Black crappie, bass, and perch are the chief fish.

A parking lot is to the left after the park entrance. The 0.8-mile *Alder*

Map display at Duke Power State Park
Courtesy of West District Office

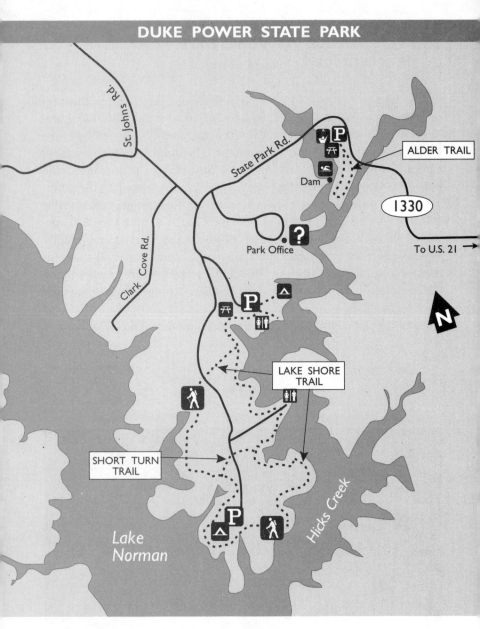

Trail begins at the parking lot of picnic area #1. It loops around the peninsula among stands of wildflowers, willow, and tag alder to picnic tables and the swimming area. (USGS map: Troutman)

Address and Access: Superintendent, Duke Power State Park, 159 Inland Sea Lane, Troutman, NC 28166 (704-528-6350). From the town of Troutman (located 6 miles south of Statesville and 3 miles north of I-77 on US-21/NC-115), go 3.6 miles west on State Park Road (SR-1330).

Support Facilities: Groceries, gasoline, and restaurant food are available in Troutman. Statesville has shopping centers, motels, and restaurants.

Lake Shore Trail

Length and Difficulty: 6.7 miles round-trip, moderate

Trailhead and Description: Begin at the parking lot of picnic area #2 and follow the sign right of the restrooms to the white blazes. At a junction after 0.5 mile, turn either right or left for a loop. If turning right, you will reach the main park road and cross near a gate. (It is 0.7 mile south on the road to the campground.) At a red-blazed junction, proceed ahead by the lakeside to the end of the peninsula. (For a shortcut, you can follow the red blazes for a 3.5-mile loop.) In the process, you will pass the amphitheater and the campground before continuing around the lakeshore on the return trip.

FORT DOBBS STATE HISTORIC SITE
Iredell County

Named for Royal Governor Arthur Dobbs, the fort was built during the French and Indian War (1754–63) to protect settlers. Excavations of the vanished fort show a moat, a cellar, a magazine area, and a well. A pioneer cottage has exhibits of the period. The 0.5-mile *Fort Dobbs Nature Trail* goes through a hardwood forest and has footbridges over small ravines. Ferns and wildflowers are prominent among the spicebush.

Address and Access: Fort Dobbs State Historic Site, Route 9, Box A-415, Statesville, NC 28677 (704-873-5866). From the junction of I-40 and US-21 in Statesville, go north 1.2 miles on US-21, turn left on Fort Dobbs Road (SR-1930), and go 1.3 miles to the entrance, on the right.

HANGING ROCK STATE PARK

Stokes County

Hanging Rock State Park boasts 6,000 acres in the Sauratown Mountains and more than 18 miles of named and side trails. They go to scenic heights, waterfall areas, rocky ridges, and caves and in the process provide the hiker with views of as many as 300 species of flora, including mountain camellia (*Stewartia ovata*). Canadian and Carolina hemlock grow together here, a rarity, and a species of lespedeza is found only in this area. Animal life includes deer, fox, skunk, woodchuck, squirrel, raccoon, owl, and hawk. The park offers camping, cabins, picnicking, swimming, fishing, and mountain climbing. All the trails connect except *Lower Cascades Trail*. It can be reached by going west from the park entrance on Moore's Springs Road (SR-1001) for 0.3 mile; turn left on Hall Road (SR-2012) and go 0.4 mile to the parking area, on the right. This 0.6-mile round-trip trail descends to the scenic falls and a pool under a huge overhang. (USGS map: Hanging Rock)

Address and Access: Superintendent, Hanging Rock State Park, P.O. Box 278, Danbury, NC 27016 (910-593-8480). To reach the park, turn off NC-8 onto Moore's Springs Road 1.5 miles north of Danbury; the turn is across the road from Reynolds Hospital. The western entrance route is off NC-66 about 0.5 mile north of the community of Gap on Moore's Springs Road.

Support Facilities: The park has a campground with family vacation cabins and 73 tent/trailer campsites without hookups. The campground is open all year; the water is turned off from December 1 to March 15. The cabins are available with reservations from March 1 to November 30. Groceries, a restaurant, gasoline, and a post office are in Danbury.

Hanging Rock Trail (*1.2 miles*)
Wolf Rock Loop Trail (*1.9 miles*)
Cook's Wall Trail (*1.1 miles*)
Magnolia Spring Trail (*0.4 mile*)
Chestnut Oak Nature Trail (*0.7 mile*)
Moore's Wall Loop Trail (*4.2 miles*)

Length and Difficulty: 11.4 miles combined round-trip, easy to strenuous

Connecting Trail: Tory's Den Trail

Special Features: Geology, wildflowers, scenic views

Trailheads and Description: After passing the park office entrance (left), turn left to a large parking lot at the visitor center. The heavily used *Hanging Rock Trail* begins on the right at a sign. Descend on wide cement steps and follow a cement treadway for 340 yards before ascending on gravel. At 0.5 mile, you will junction with *Wolf Rock Loop Trail*, to the right. At Hanging Rock, you will ascend steeply for 200 feet on metamorphic rock to the summit for superb views. Backtrack to form a loop by taking *Wolf Rock Loop Trail*. You will ascend to and remain on a rocky ridge featuring pine, oak, laurel, and blueberry. Overlooks on the left face southeast and south. After 1 mile, you will junction with *Cook's Wall Trail*, which goes ahead on the ridge. *Wolf Rock Loop Trail* turns sharply right, descends to join *Chestnut Oak Nature Trail*, and ends at the swimming lake's bathhouse. From here through the parking lot and the entrance road, it is 0.4 mile back to the parking lot for *Hanging Rock Trail*, for a loop of 4.2 miles.

If continuing on the ridge crest for *Cook's Wall Trail*, you will ascend among a mixture of hardwoods, pine, and laurel with patches of galax, trailing arbutus, and downy false foxglove. After 0.5 mile, you will junction with *Magnolia Spring Trail*, on the right. (Although this name may not be on the trail signs, the trail is a popular connector between the park's two main ridges. It received its name from the magnolia growing in a damp area of the trial's northern end.) You will arrive at House Rock at 0.7 mile. Here are excellent views of Hanging Rock to the northeast and the vicinity of Winston-Salem to the south. At 1.1 miles, you will reach Devil's Chimney over rocky Cook's Wall for a view of Pilot Mountain to the west. Backtrack, but turn left at *Magnolia Spring Trail*. You will descend steeply through a dense forest to Magnolia Spring at 0.1 mile, then pass through an arbor of rhododendron, cross a footbridge over a clear stream, and junction with *Moore's Wall Loop Trail* (right and left) at 0.4 mile. A right turn leads through a bog with boardwalks. Ferns and purple turtlehead grow nearby. You will then junction with *Chestnut Oak Nature Trail*, arrive at the bathhouse, and return to the *Hanging Rock Trail* parking lot, for a loop of 6.4 miles.

If following *Moore's Wall Loop Trail* from *Magnolia Spring Trail*, follow the sign; after 0.6 mile, you will junction with a connector to the former *Sauratown Trail* and *Tory's Den Trail*. Turn right and ascend to a rocky area with hemlock, turkey grass, and laurel after another 0.6 mile. You will reach an observation tower (2,579 feet in elevation) offering spectacular views at 1.9 miles. You will then descend and pass Balanced Rock and Indian Face on an old road. You will cross Cascade Creek at 3 miles, pass through the camping area, and rejoin the trail's entrance. Turn left and return to the parking lot at the bathhouse at 3.9 miles. If walking from this parking lot to the Hanging Rock parking lot, the loop is 9.3 miles; if hiking only *Moore's Wall Loop Trail*, it is 4.2 miles if you begin at the parking lot at the bathhouse.

Upper Cascades Trail *(0.2 mile)*
Indian Creek Trail *(3.7 miles)*

Length and Difficulty: 7.8 miles combined round-trip, easy to moderate

Special Features: Waterfalls, wildlife, cliffs

Trailheads and Description: From the visitor center parking lot and the picnic area, access *Upper Cascades Trail* at the west side of the parking lot. Part of the trail is asphalt and is suitable for the physically handicapped. Backtrack.

To access *Indian Creek Trail*, follow the trail signs at the northeast end of the parking lot and the picnic area. Descend 0.4 mile to a shady area at Hidden Falls on Indian Creek. Continue downstream, crossing the creek several times. You will pass a junction (left) with a connector trail to a group camping area. Cross the creek to exit at Moore's Springs Road at 1.7 miles (0.1 mile east of the park entrance).

Cross the road, descend on an old farm road, cross a cement bridge, pass left of an old tobacco barn, and descend to the creek. You will then veer away from the creek, ascend a ridge, follow an old forest road, and descend to a scenic overlook from cliffs at 2.9 miles. Descend to the creek's basin near cliff walls, over mossy banks, and through dense rhododendron. After several creek crossings, you will arrive at an old farm road. Turn right and cross the creek on a footbridge to the trail's end. Ahead, it is 0.1 mile to the *Dan River Canoe Trail* boat-launching and parking area. Backtrack or use a second vehicle. (To access the river by vehicle from the park entrance, drive 0.5 mile east on Hanging Rock Road to Piedmont Springs Road—SR-1489—on the left. After 0.9 mile,

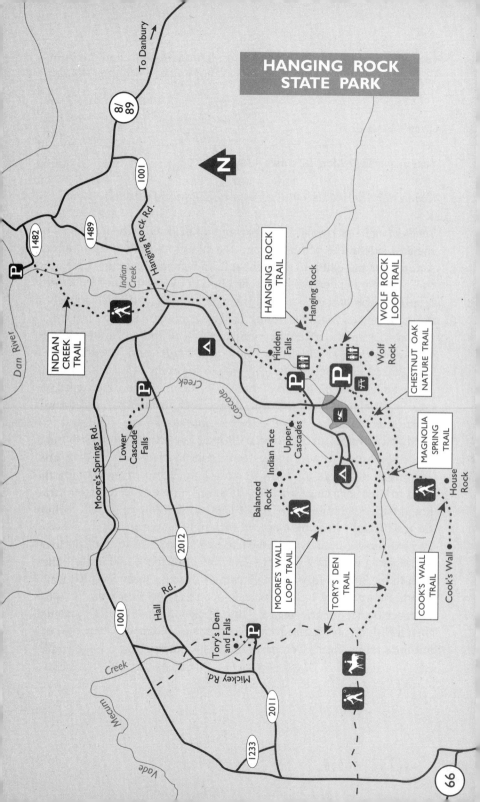

HANGING ROCK
STATE PARK

To Danbury

8/89

1001

1482

1489

Hanging Rock Rd.

Indian Creek

N

P

INDIAN CREEK TRAIL

Dan River

HANGING ROCK TRAIL

Hanging Rock

WOLF ROCK LOOP TRAIL

Hidden Falls

Wolf Rock

P

P

CHESTNUT OAK NATURE TRAIL

Cascade Creek

MAGNOLIA SPRING TRAIL

P

Moore's Springs Rd.

Lower Cascade Falls

Indian Face

Upper Cascades

House Rock

Balanced Rock

2012

MOORE'S WALL LOOP TRAIL

TORY'S DEN TRAIL

COOK'S WALL TRAIL

Cook's Wall

Hall Rd.

1001

Tory's Den and Falls

P

Mickey Rd.

Creek

Mecum

Vade

2011

1233

66

turn left on NC-8/89, go 0.3 mile, turn left on SR-1482, and go 0.4 mile to the trailhead at the creek. The river parking area is on the right.)

Tory's Den Trail

Length and Difficulty: 4.2 miles, easy

Connecting Trails: Chestnut Oak Nature Trail, Moore's Wall Loop Trail

Trailhead and Description: From parking lot #2, follow the trail signs on the east side of the bathhouse and the lakeshore. Follow *Chestnut Oak Nature Trail,* but exit it to the right at 0.3 mile and follow the red-blazed trail. At 0.4 mile, you will pass a junction to the right with *Moore's Wall Loop Trail.* You will cross a stream and boardwalk and reach a junction on the left with *Magnolia Spring Trail* at 1 mile. (*Magnolia Spring Trail* ascends 0.4 mile to a junction with *Cook's Wall Trail.*) Continue ahead. You will ascend slightly to a saddle at 1.5 miles and junction with a blue-blazed trail on the left. (The trail to the right is *Moore's Wall Loop Trail.*) Follow the blue-blazed trail. After 0.5 mile, you will reach the crest of Huckleberry Ridge near a large rock formation. Descend to a junction at 2.4 miles with the former *Sauratown Trail,* right and left. (*Sauratown Trail* is an abandoned 19-mile horse trail. Efforts are being made to reopen it, with its eastern trailhead elsewhere in the park.) Turn right and descend. You will cross a small stream at 3.5 miles. Ascend to Charlie Young Road (SR-2028) at 3.6 miles and turn right. Follow the road 0.4 mile to the Tory's Den parking lot, on the left. Follow the trail 0.3 mile to an outcrop, but turn right on the approach. Descend 90 yards near a small cave to the left; turn right. (Ahead to the left, it is a few yards to a view of Tory's Den Falls.) Descend 100 yards on the path to the 30-foot Tory's Den. Backtrack or use a second vehicle at the Tory's Den parking lot. For vehicle access, drive west from the park entrance on Moore's Springs Road to Mickey Road (SR-2011); turn left, then left again on Charlie Young Road; the total distance from the park entrance to the Tory's Den parking lot is 4.3 miles.

MORROW MOUNTAIN STATE PARK

Stanly County

This 4,693-acre park is in the heart of the lower Piedmont region and in the ancient Uwharrie range. More than 500 million years ago, it was covered by a shallow sea in which volcanic islands developed; they

View of Lake Tillery from Morrow Mountain
Photo courtesy of Morrow Mountain State Park

later became the hard basalt and rhyolite deposits of this area. Established in 1935, the park is on the Pee Dee River and Lake Tillery. Named after J. M. Morrow, a former landowner, the park is scenic and historic. The restored homestead of Dr. Francis Kron—a former CCC camp and a historic site in its own right—is an example of the park's effort to maintain both cultural and natural resources. The park offers a nature museum, picnicking, boating, fishing, nature programs, swimming, hiking, equestrian trails, and camping. The 106 tent/RV campsites for family camping are open all year. Water, showers, and restrooms are available at the campground, but hookups are not; the water is turned off from December 1 to mid-March. Backpack camping and youth-group tent camping are offered, but advance registration is necessary. Rental cabins, available from March 1 through November, also require advance registration. (USGS maps: Badin, Morrow Mountain)

Address and Access: Superintendent, Morrow Mountain State Park, 49104 Morrow Mountain Road, Albemarle, NC 28001 (704-982-4402). From the junction of NC-740 and NC-24/27/73 in Albemarle, drive 1.8 miles northeast on NC-740 to Morrow Mountain Road (SR-1798), then go 2.5 miles to the park entrance.

Laurel Trail *(0.6 mile)*
Morrow Mountain Trail *(3 miles)*
Quarry Trail *(0.6 mile)*
Hattaway Mountain Trail *(2 miles)*

Length and Difficulty: 6.2 miles combined, easy to moderate

Trailheads and Description: Park at the Natural History Museum and begin *Laurel Trail* behind the museum. If going clockwise, stay on the main trail through a mature forest of hardwoods, pine, laurel, and pink azalea for a loop of 0.6 mile. (After 0.2 mile, you will reach a junction to the left with *Morrow Mountain Trail*, which goes to the top of Morrow Mountain, 936 feet in elevation. Ascend west of Sugarloaf Creek to a junction with *Sugarloaf Mountain Trail* at 0.7 mile. Follow *Sugarloaf Mountain Trail* for 0.6 mile and turn left. You will cross a small stream and arrive at the east side of Morrow Mountain at 2.5 miles. You will then ascend steeply on a switchback to a junction with *Mountain Loop Trail*. Exit at either the overlook or the picnic area to the Morrow Mountain parking area.)

For *Quarry Trail*, hike northwest from the museum and go past the

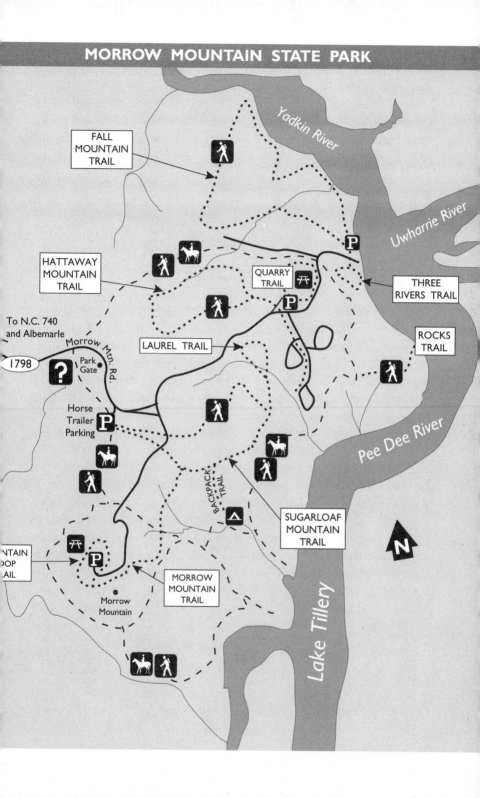

swimming pool to the picnic area, or simply drive to the picnic parking area. The loop of 0.6 mile reveals a man-made gorge where volcanic slate of the Slate Belt can be studied.

Begin *Hattaway Mountain Trail* at the pool bathhouse and follow the 2-mile loop trail up and over dry, rocky Hattaway Mountain, the park's third-highest. The mature forest has oak, sourwood, maple, and laurel.

Three Rivers Trail *(0.6 mile)*
Fall Mountain Trail *(4.15 miles)*

Length and Difficulty: 4.7 miles combined, easy to moderate

Special Features: Kron House, river views, rhyolite

Trailheads and Description: Park at the boathouse near the boat launch. *Fall Mountain Trail* begins at the south end of the parking lot. If taking the western route, you will junction left with *Three Rivers Trail*. (*Three Rivers Trail* is a 0.6-mile self-guided interpretive trail that crosses the boat-launch road and loops by an open marsh of swamp rose and arrowwood. It passes through a damp forest area to the riverside for views of the Yadkin, Pee Dee, and Uwharrie Rivers.) Continuing on *Fall Mountain Trail*, you will twice cross an access path to the youth-group tent campsites. At 1.2 miles, you will pass the historic Kron House, to the left. Dr. Kron, a physician, lived here from 1834 until his death in 1883; his 6,000-acre farm was used for numerous horticultural experiments. Ascend north to cross the Fall Mountain ridge in a forest of oak, laurel, and scattered pine at 1.7 miles. You will then descend a rough area of rhyolite and volcanic outcrops. There are excellent views of Falls Dam and the Yadkin River. Silver bell, coneflower, and lip fern are among the flowering plants and ferns. You will pass through a crack in a boulder the size of a house. You will then descend, cross a small stream, and twice cross the road to the group camp, for a loop of 4.1 miles. You may see deer and squirrel in these areas.

Rocks Trail

Length and Difficulty: 2.6 miles round-trip, easy

Trailhead and Description: Park at the administrative building and begin at the rear of the building, hiking east. You will arrive at the family campground. Follow the yellow blazes on *Rocks Trail*, which includes parts of a bridle trail. Turn left 0.2 mile from the campground. (Because of numerous campground trails and extra lead-in trails to *Mountain Creek Bridle Trail*, hikers may need to watch carefully for the yellow blazes.) You will pass right of a junction with the bridle trail at 0.6 mile. Continue ahead to an excellent view of the Pee Dee River. You will descend over a rocky area to the trail's end at 1.3 miles. Return by the same route.

Sugarloaf Mountain Trail *(2.8 miles)*
Mountain Loop Trail *(0.8 mile)*

Length and Difficulty: 3.6 miles combined, moderate

Trailheads and Description: These trails connect with *Morrow Mountain Trail*, bridle trails, and Morrow Mountain Road. Park at the lot to the right (east) of the staff residences. Follow the trail sign for hikers, bearing left from the bridle trail. You will cross two small streams and Morrow Mountain Road. Ascend and follow the northwest ridge of Sugarloaf Mountain (858 feet in elevation). You will reach a junction to the left with *Morrow Mountain Trail* at 1.4 miles. Turn right jointly with *Morrow Mountain Trail*. After 2 miles, continue to the right. (*Morrow Mountain Trail* goes left in its ascent to the top of Morrow Mountain.) You will cross Morrow Mountain Road at 2.2 miles, cross a stream at 2.7 miles, and enter a field near the parking lot to complete the loop.

For *Mountain Loop Trail*, drive to the top of Morrow Mountain. The trailhead can be found at the picnic shelter or the overlook. It leads to a loop around the peak. The trail is graded and has bridges over the ravines. It connects on the east side with *Morrow Mountain Trail*, described above. From Morrow Mountain, hikers can enjoy views to the east of Lake Tillery and Dennis Mountain (the route of *Uwharrie Trail*) in Uwharrie National Forest. For information on the national forest, see chapter 1.

PILOT MOUNTAIN STATE PARK

Surry and Yadkin Counties

Pilot Mountain State Park covers 3,703 acres in two sections—Pilot Mountain and the south and north sides of the Yadkin River. The sections are connected by a 6.5-mile, 300-foot-wide forest corridor for hikers and equestrians. In the park is Big Pinnacle, which rises 200 feet from its base, 1,500 feet above the valley floor, and 2,420 feet above sea level. Dedicated a national natural landmark in 1976, it is geologically a quartzite monadnock.

Park activities include canoe camping, picnicking, horseback riding, hiking, and camping. A family tent/trailer campground is near the base of the north side of the mountain; it has hot showers but no hookups and is closed December 1 through March 15. The trails connect easily, with the exception of *Yadkin River Trail* on the south side of the Yadkin River. *Sauratown Trail* has its western terminus at the park, and *Mountains-to-Sea Trail* will pass through *Corridor Trail*. (USGS maps: Pinnacle, Siloam)

Address and Access: Superintendent, Pilot Mountain State Park, Route 3, Box 21, Pinnacle, NC 27043 (910-325-2355). The entrance to the park is at the junction of US-52 and Pilot Knob Road (SR-2053) 14 miles south of Mount Airy and 24 miles north of Winston-Salem.

Sassafras Trail *(0.5 mile)*
Jomeokee Trail *(0.8 mile)*
Ledge Spring Trail *(1.6 miles)*
Mountain Trail *(2.5 miles)*
Grindstone Trail *(1.6 miles)*

Length and Difficulty: 7 miles combined, easy to strenuous

Special Features: Big Pinnacle, scenic ledges

Trailheads and Description: All of these trails connect and can be reached from the parking lot at the top of the mountain. From the parking lot, go past and behind the comfort station to a rocky area and a sign for *Jomeokee Trail.* Thirty yards to the left is *Sassafras Trail.* (*Sassafras Trail*

Pilot Mountain State Park

leads north on a self-guided loop. It is an interpretive trail among pitch pine, chestnut oak, laurel, and ground-cover patches of galax.) At the *Jomeokee Trail* sign, descend among rocks and follow a much-used access to Big Pinnacle. *Jomeokee* is an Indian word for "great guide" or

PILOT MOUNTAIN STATE PARK

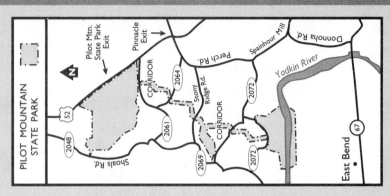

PILOT MOUNTAIN STATE PARK

NORTH AREA

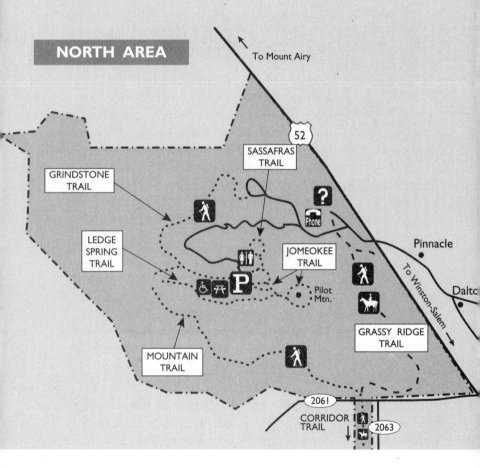

To Mount Airy

52

SASSAFRAS TRAIL

GRINDSTONE TRAIL

Phone

Pinnacle

LEDGE SPRING TRAIL

JOMEOKEE TRAIL

Pilot Mtn.

To Winston-Salem

Dalto

P

MOUNTAIN TRAIL

GRASSY RIDGE TRAIL

2061

CORRIDOR TRAIL

2063

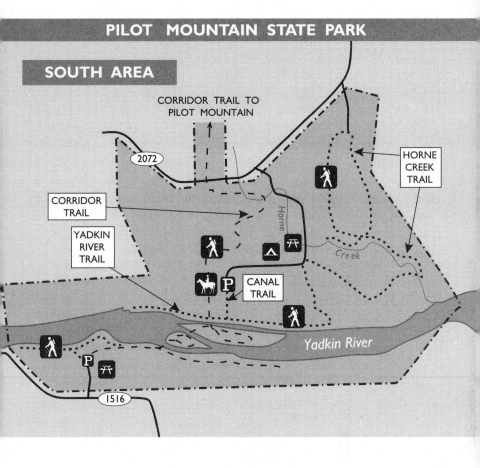

SOUTH AREA

CORRIDOR TRAIL TO
PILOT MOUNTAIN

2072

HORNE
CREEK
TRAIL

CORRIDOR
TRAIL

YADKIN
RIVER
TRAIL

Horne

Creek

CANAL
TRAIL

P

Yadkin River

P

1516

"pilot." At 0.2 mile, you will pass the base of Little Pinnacle and reach a junction to the right with the yellow-blazed *Ledge Spring Trail*. Continue ahead. After another 0.1 mile, turn right to follow a rocky loop around Big Pinnacle. The trail walls have caves, eroded rock formations, ferns, wildflowers, lichens, and mosses. Park officials say that ravens nest on the summit. Climbing and rappelling are prohibited. On your return from the loop, take *Ledge Spring Trail*, to the left. You will descend on a rocky, rough, and sometimes strenuous course to the base of the ledges. At 1 mile, you will reach Ledge Spring (right), located 30 yards from the junction with *Mountain Trail*. (Formerly *Mountain Bridle Trail*, *Mountain Trail* is a rough, red-blazed connector trail to *Corridor Trail*, described below. It descends through a hardwood forest with scattered patches of laurel and pine at the beginning. At 1.8 miles, it reaches large boulders pushed up in a row from a former clearing. After another 0.4 mile, it leaves the row and follows a footpath to an exit at Surry Line Road— SR-2061. It junctions left with the 1.7-mile *Grassy Ridge Trail* and right with the 6.5-mile *Corridor Trail* at 2.5 miles.) To continue on *Ledge Spring Trail*, turn right and begin a steep ascent over the ledges to a junction on the left with *Grindstone Trail* at 1.3 miles. (*Grindstone Trail* first follows an easy contour but soon descends in a rocky area with hardwoods and laurel. It crosses a footbridge and small stream at 1.3 miles, crosses an old road at 1.5 miles, and exits at 1.6 miles between campsites #16 and #17.) Continue the ascent ahead on *Ledge Spring Trail*. You will pass to the right of the picnic area and return to the southwest corner of the parking lot at 1.5 miles.

Grassy Ridge Trail *(1.7 miles)*
Corridor Trail *(6.5 miles)*
Horne Creek Trail *(1.3 miles)*
Canal Trail *(1 mile round-trip)*

Length and Difficulty: 10.5 miles combined, easy

Trailheads and Description: With the exception of *Canal Trail*, these are equestrian/hiker trails. The northern terminus of the white-blazed *Grassy Ridge Trail* is on Pilot Knob Road (SR-1151) in Surry County under the US-52 bridge 0.2 mile east of the park entrance. At this trailhead is the western terminus of the planned *Sauratown Trail*. For vehicular access to the south end of *Grassy Ridge Trail* and the north end of *Corridor Trail* from here, drive east on Pilot Knob Road 1.1 miles to the junction with Old Winston Road (SR-1152). Turn right, go 0.4 mile, and turn right on Old US-52 (SR-1236). After another 0.4 mile, turn right across the railroad on Surry Line Road (SR-1148), which becomes Pinnacle Hotel Road (SR-2061) in Surry County; drive 1.6 miles.

You will enter *Grassy Ridge Trail* at a poplar tree and proceed into a hardwood forest. You will cross a streamlet at 0.1 mile and reach a junction on the right at 0.2 mile. (To the right, it is 0.3 mile on a footpath to the park office.) Continue left. You will pass an old tobacco barn at 0.4 mile and cross small streams at 0.5 mile and 1.3 miles. You will arrive at Pinnacle Hotel Road (SR-2061 in Surry County) at 1.7 miles. (To the right on the road, it is 75 yards to the southern terminus of the red-blazed *Mountain Trail*.) Cross the road to a junction with Culler Road (SR-2063) and a parking area in the corner of Pilot Mountain State Park Corridor. Here is the northern terminus of *Corridor Trail*. (For vehicular access to the southern terminus of *Corridor Trail*, drive west on SR-2061 for 2.6 miles to the junction with Shoals Road—SR-2048. Turn left and go south for 4 miles; turn neither right nor left but travel partly on SR-2069, also called Shoals Road, to a fork. Ahead is a dead-end sign. Turn left on the gravel Hauser Road—SR-2072—and go 1 mile to the southern terminus, on the left. Ahead, it is 0.2 mile to the park's Yadkin River section, on the right.)

Begin the yellow-blazed *Corridor Trail* on an old farm road in a grove of Virginia pine. You will pass under a power line at 0.1 mile. At 0.3 mile is a view (looking back) of the pinnacles. You will then cross two footbridges with a meadow of wildflowers and elderberry between them. At 0.7 mile, you will leave the forest and enter a field that offers another good view of the pinnacles (looking backward). After 0.1 mile, you will enter a forest of pine and cedar. You will pass remnants of an old tobacco barn on the left at 1.2 miles, then cross a small stream bordered with pinxter at 1.4 miles and another stream at 1.5 miles. At 1.6 miles, you will cross the paved Mount Zion Road (SR-2064). Follow the trail through old farmland and young-growth forest. You will descend to rock-hop a tributary of Grassy Creek at 2.6 miles. You will pass patches of yellow root and wood betony among the river birch, then exit from the woods into an open area of honeysuckle, blackberry, and poison ivy, then cross the paved Shoals Road (SR-2048) at 3 miles. Follow the woods' edge into the forest, cross a stream, cross a number of old woods roads, and descend gently to another stream with beds of sensitive fern at 4.7 miles. You will cross a footbridge constructed by the Young Adult Conservation Corps, then cross the paved Stony Ridge Church Road (SR-2070) at 5 miles. Follow the trail through alternating pine groves and open hardwoods. At 6 miles, you will cross a rocky tributary of Horne Creek; upstream are two large millstones. You will pass under a power line at 6.3 miles and reach the trail's southern terminus at Hauser Road (SR-2072) at 6.5 miles. *Horne Creek Trail* begins across the road. (To the left on the road, it is 0.2 mile to the entrance, on the right, of the Yadkin River section of the park at a log shed. For vehicular access to US-52 from here, drive east on SR-2072 for 2.8 miles to Perch Road—SR-2065. Turn left and go 3.5 miles to US-52 in Pinnacle. Vehicular access to the southern end of *Horne Creek Trail* is on the park road. Drive in at the park gate by the log shed, ford the small Horne Creek three times, and pass through a picnic area. You will reach a cul-de-sac on a bluff by the Yadkin River. *Canal Trail* begins on the west side of the cul-de-sac at a wide trail opening and connects with *Horne Creek Trail* at the Southern Railroad track after 80 yards.)

At the northern end of *Horne Creek Trail*, you will enter a field featuring scattered walnut trees. After 0.3 mile, you will arrive at the park road. Turn right, rock-hop Horne Creek, and reenter the woods at 0.5 mile. You will ascend and rejoin the park road in a grove of pine at 0.8 mile. Turn right and follow the road, but leave it after 0.2 mile. Descend to the Southern Railroad track and junction left with *Canal Trail*. (*Canal Trail* begins 80 yards up the bank to the cul-de-sac.) Cross the railroad tracks. After 60 yards, you will reach the Yadkin River, the trail's end. (To the right, *Canal Trail* crosses a footbridge. It goes upstream 0.5 mile between the river and the railroad tracks among sycamore, poplar, and river birch. At 0.2 mile, you will pass a long rock wall to the right. Backtrack.) Although *Horne Creek Trail* ends at the Yadkin, horses can ford the river to two islands and to *Yadkin River Trail*, described below.

Yadkin River Trail

Length and Difficulty: 0.7 mile, easy

Trailhead and Description: To reach this trail, take NC-67 to East Bend and follow Old NC-67 (SR-1545) into town. Turn northwest on Fairground Road (SR-1541), go 0.5 mile, turn right on Shady Grove Church Road (SR-1538), drive 0.4 mile, turn right on Old Shoals Road (SR-1546), and go 2.5 miles to the picnic and parking area. Follow the yellow-blazed trail to the river and return on a loop through a pine forest west of the ranger station. This is also an area for a bridle trail that crosses the Yadkin River north to *Horne Creek Trail* and *Corridor Trail*, described above. There are two renovated campsites for individual canoeists on the 45-acre islands in the Yadkin River. Group camping is not permitted.

RENDEZVOUS MOUNTAIN EDUCATIONAL STATE FOREST

Wilkes County

In 1926, Judge Thomas Finely donated the 142-acre Rendezvous Mountain to the state as a park, but the state never developed it. Thirty years later, it became a state forest. It is a scenic hardwood forest with rugged terrain at the foothills of the Blue Ridge Mountains. It offers facilities for picnicking, hiking, and nature study; facilities for primitive camping are planned.

After entering the gate, park at the first parking lot on the right. Cross the road to the right of the picnic area and follow the 0.2-mile *Table Mountain Pine Sawmill Trail*. This loop has historic exhibits of timber-cutting equipment and logging methods, as well as a sawmill from the 1950s. At the second parking lot on the right, the 0.6-mile *Rendezvous Mountain Talking Tree Trail* loops through a beautiful forest of hardwoods, laurel, pinxter, and flame azalea with scattered rhododendron. The descent is moderate to steep. Also beginning at the parking lot is the 275-yard *Firetower Trail*, which ascends north past the forest office to the old fire tower (2,445 feet in elevation) and its scenic views. (USGS map: Purlear)

Address and Access: Forest Supervisor, Rendezvous Mountain Educational State Forest, Box 42, Purlear, NC 28665 (910-667-5072). From NC-16 in Millers Creek (5.3 miles northwest of Wilkesboro), turn west on Old US-421 (SR-1304) and go 2.8 miles to the junction with Purlear Road (SR-1346). Turn right on Purlear Road and go 1.8 miles, then turn left on Rendezvous Mountain Road (SR-1348) and ascend to the forest entrance after 1.3 miles.

Students on the Cedarock Trail in Alamance County

Chapter 3

TRAILS IN COUNTY PARKS

───────────────

Fifty-nine of the state's 100 counties have parks and recreation departments. They operate as a separate public unit in each county, usually under a board of county commissioners. A few counties and cities combine their departments or resources to provide joint services or special projects. Examples are Clinton and Sampson County and Mocksville and Davie County. Because of population needs and available funding, county parks vary in size, facilities, and scope, from simple day-use picnic areas to complex recreational centers such as Tanglewood Park in Forsyth County.

When the President's Commission on Americans Outdoors reported its findings in 1986, it showed rapid expansion in a number of North Carolina cities. With an increase in population and less space in the cities for outdoor recreation, county parks are becoming more vital for green space. The report also showed a demographic trend toward a fast-growing older segment of the population and a desire for recreation close to home. Mecklenburg and Forsyth are examples of counties preparing for this trend. Mecklenburg's diverse park and greenway system, the largest in the state, will become what Elisabeth Hair, former chair of the board of county commissioners, called "Charlotte's green necklace." In Forsyth County, greenways will connect the county's towns to a greenway network in the city of Winston-Salem. A number of county parks and recreation departments have constructed physical-fitness trails. Others, such as Craven County's department, do not own property but maintain exercise trails on public-school property.

To receive the *North Carolina Parks and Recreation Directory*, which contains listings for the state's counties and cities with parks, contact the Division of Parks and Recreation, Box 27687, Raleigh, NC 27687 (919-733-PARK), or call 919-515-7118 at North Carolina State University.

ALAMANCE COUNTY

The Alamance County Recreation and Parks Department is well known for its scenic and splendid network of 150 miles of bicycle trail routes. Among its seven trails is *Route 74*, a 59-mile route that circles the county and connects with all the other bike routes. Plans may be to connect the loop with *Mountains-to-Sea Trail* in the northern part of the county. *Mountains-to-Sea Bike Route #2* passes through the southern part of the county on its way from Murphy to Manteo. The county's bicycle trails were planned to connect historic sites and parks, one of which is described below. For information, contact the Recreation and Parks Department, 217 College Street, Graham, NC 27253 (910-570-6760, office; 910-570-6759, camp reservations).

Cedarock Park

This historic and highly diversified 414-acre park contains the Cedarock Park Center, used for conferences and workshops in the Paul Stevens homestead, and Cedarock Historical Farm, dating from the 1830s. Recreational facilities include two disk golf courses; basketball and volleyball courts; picnic areas, some with shelters; a fishing pond; walk-in campsites for primitive camping (permits are required); a ropes obstacle course; playgrounds; and a variety of trails. The 4.3-mile *Equestrian Trail* circles the perimeter of the park. On the northwest side of the circle is the 0.25-mile *Hiking Trail* near the Wellspring Disk Golf Course. Access to the horse trail is near Cedarock Historical Farm. A parking area near picnic shelter #3 gives access to the 1.3-mile *Mountain Bike Trail*. Color-coded interconnecting trail loops are described below. The park is open all year. (USGS map: Snow Camp)

Access: From the junction of I-85/40 and NC-49 in Burlington (exit 145A from the west, exit 145 from the east), go nearly 6 miles on NC-49 to the junction with Friendship-Patterson Mill Road; turn left. Drive 0.3 mile to the park entrance, on the left. The ranger station is at the first house on the right, the Garrett homestead.

Cedarock Trail *(2.2 miles)*
Ecology Trail *(0.5 mile)*
Nature Trail *(0.8 mile)*
Green Trail *(0.13 mile)*
Red Trail *(0.16 mile)*

Length and Difficulty: 3.9 miles combined, easy

Trailheads and Description: From the picnic area parking lot, begin at shelter #3 at the trail signboard. (To the right is the white-blazed *Mountain Bike Trail*, which descends to a fork after 75 yards. Hiking in either direction takes you to a meadow and a footbridge over Rock Creek. A loop entirely in the forest follows.)

Begin the yellow-blazed *Cedarock Trail* to the left of the trail signboard. The trail descends to cross a narrow footbridge over Rock Creek at 0.1 mile in a meadow of wildflowers. After a few yards, you will enter a forest and junction with the brown-blazed *Ecology Trail* to the left; this trail runs jointly with *Cedarock Trail* for a distance. At 0.4 mile, *Ecology Trail* turns left to complete its loop. Along the way, it skirts a bend of Rock Creek.

To the right is the blue-blazed *Nature Trail*. If following it, look for *Green Trail* to the right after a few yards; *Green Trail* makes a short curve among ferns, wild azalea, and rock formations beside a cascading stream. Turn left and return to *Nature Trail*. (In the short distance between the trailheads of *Green Trail*, *Nature Trail* junctions with the western trailhead of *Red Trail*, a connector.) Continue upstream on *Nature Trail*; you will pass through an oak/hickory forest among scattered pine. Ferns, hepatica, and wild orchid are prominent near the stream. At 0.4 mile, you will leave the scenic stream and ascend gently over a ridge. You will junction left with *Red Trail* to a walk-in campsite at 0.6 mile, then cross a small footbridge and rejoin *Cedarock Trail* at 0.7 mile.

If taking a left, you will rock-hop a small stream and junction with *Ecology Trail* for a return to the trail signboard. If continuing to the right on *Cedarock Trail*, you will soon leave the forest, cross through a meadow

CEDAROCK PARK

CEDAROCK TRAIL

Old Mill Site and Rock Dam

NATURE TRAIL

RED TRAIL

ECOLOGY TRAIL

GREEN TRAIL

Rock Creek

P

P

P

Garrett House Trail Rd.
(NOT AN ENTRANCE)

Basketball Courts

Volleyball Courts

To Burlington and I-85

49

Cedarock Park Road 2409

Gate

Friendship- Patterson Mill Rd.

1130

Rock Creek

To Mount Herman and Rock Creek Rd.

near a tent campground, reenter the forest, and reach an old mill dam on the left. You will then cross *Equestrian Trail* and a bridge at Elmo's Crossing. You will enter a meadow of wildflowers, including star-of-Bethlehem (*Ipheion uniflorum*), at 2 miles. After crossing a bridge over a small stream, you will pass a maintenance area, reach the park road, and return to the parking lot near picnic shelter #3 at 2.2 miles.

FORSYTH COUNTY

Forsyth County's parks and recreation system offers 10 recreation areas and historic sites that encircle the city of Winston-Salem. It provides various programs for children and adults and special programs for the physically handicapped and senior citizens. The county's system has an excellent record of planning and working with the parks and recreation services of the city of Winston-Salem. An example is the network of bicycle routes throughout the city and county. Short and easy walking trails are located at Walkertown Community Park, Union Cross Park, Joanie Moser Memorial Park, and C. G. Hill Memorial Park. Other parks and trails are described below.

Address: Director, Parks and Recreation Department, 500 West Fourth Street, Winston-Salem, NC 27101 (910-727-2946)

Horizons Park

This 492-acre park has picnic shelters, tables with grills, restrooms, a softball field, a sand volleyball court, a playground, an 18-hole disk golf course (the state's first), and a hiking trail. (USGS map: Walkertown)

Access: One access is from the junction of US-52 and NC-8 north of the city. Follow NC-8 for 4.2 miles, turn right on Memorial Industrial School Drive (SR-1920), and drive 1.1 miles to the entrance, on the right.

Horizons Hiking Trail

Length and Difficulty: 2.5 miles combined, easy

Trailhead and Description: From the parking area, go to the picnic shelter and locate the trail signs. After 110 yards, *Horizons Hiking Trail* goes right and left for a shorter loop (loop B) and a longer loop (loop A). If going right, you will cross a stream at 0.3 mile and reach a junction with loop B to the left at 0.4 mile. If going right, you will pass through a field, cross a bridge (one of a number on the trail), and follow the white blazes. You will pass a tree nursery, cross another bridge, and begin ascending and descending on rolling hills in a young forest. Redbud, Virginia pine, dogwood, and red cedar coexist with the major hardwoods. At 1.1 miles, you will cross a boardwalk in a damp area. You will arrive at the loop B junction (left and right) at 2.1 miles. If continuing right, you will reach a huge holly tree at 2.3 miles on the right; here also is a 19th-century graveyard. Return to the nature trail to complete the loops at 2.5 miles.

Tanglewood Park

Tanglewood, the memorial park of William and Kate B. Reynolds, is an outstanding recreation and leisure resort. The park offers the elegant manor house and lodge, rustic vacation cottages, a wedding chapel, a full-service campground, a restaurant, tennis courts, a swimming pool, a 36-hole championship golf course, a driving range, a lake for paddleboats and canoes, picnic areas, bike routes, an arboretum and rose garden, a deer park, horse stables, a steeplechase course, a 0.8-mile exercise/walking trail near the campground entrance, professional summer-stock theater, and Walden Nature Center. In addition, there is a 4-mile tract for the Festival of Lights, a holiday spectacular usually held from the second week in November to the second week in January. (USGS maps: Clemmons, Advance)

Address and Access: Tanglewood Park, Box 1040, Clemmons, NC 27012. The telephone number at the welcome center is 910-778-6300; the number at the lodge is 910-778-6370; the numbers at the administrative office and Walden Nature Center are 910-778-6333 and 910-778-6342. From I-40, exit 184 (Clemmons), go south 0.9 mile on Middlebrook Drive (SR-1103) to US-158. Turn right, go 1.3 miles to Nature Trail Drive, and turn left to the entrance to the administrative building and Walden Nature Center, opposite Harper Road (SR-1101). The main park entrance and welcome center are on the left another 0.4 mile west on US-158.

Walden Nature Trail

Length and Difficulty: 1.5 miles combined, easy

Trailhead and Description: From the park entrance, go east on US-158 for 0.4 mile to the park office and Walden Nature Center, located on the right opposite Harper Road. Approach *Walden Nature Trail* behind the park office; you can acquire a pamphlet at the signboard or from the park office. The trail has three sections, each increasing in difficulty and species variety. *Little Walden Trail* (section 1, 195 yards), laid out around a small pond, offers audio stations for the visually handicapped; assistance from the park staff is available by advance reservation. *Emerson's Walk* (section 2, 0.7 mile round-trip), a paved, old road with 18 tree interpretive markers, is accessible to the physically handicapped. *Thoreau's Woods Trail* (section 3, 0.7 mile round-trip) has 28 interpretive markers about trees.

Walden Nature Trail is named after Henry David Thoreau's Walden Pond. It was completed in 1982 as a memorial to the North Carolina wildlife enforcement officers who have died in the line of duty since 1947. *Little Walden Trail* was built entirely by volunteers and through donations. Major contributors were the Reader's Digest Foundation, the Winston-Salem Host Lions Club, the AT&T Pioneers, and Girl Scout Troop 437. There is an exhibit of live wildlife to the left of the main trailhead.

ROWAN COUNTY

Dan Nicholas Park

Successful business executive and philanthropist Dan Nicholas donated 330 acres to Rowan County in 1968 for recreational activities. As a result, the county commissioners established a parks and recreation board to develop and administer this park. Facilities include areas for fishing, picnicking (with shelters), tennis, paddleboating, full-service camping, and hiking. The park also offers four ball fields; a craft shop; a nature center with plant, animal, and geological exhibits; a small zoo; and the outdoor T. M. Stanback Theater. The park is open all year. (USGS map: Salisbury)

Address and Access: Director, Parks and Recreation Department, Route 10, Box 832, Salisbury, NC 28144 (704-636-2089). From the junction of I-85 and East Spencer, take Choate Road (SR-2125) 1.1 miles east. Turn left on McCandless Road, which becomes Bringle Ferry Road (SR-1002) after 0.5 mile. Continue east 4.8 miles to the park entrance, on the left.

Persimmon Branch Trail *(2.3 miles)*
Lake Trail *(1 mile)*

Length and Difficulty: 3.3 miles combined, easy

Trailheads and Description: From the concession stand at the dam, walk to the opposite side of the lake and turn right at 0.2 mile on *Persimmon Branch Trail.* Follow the 32 interpretive markers that identify trees such as oak, pine, ash, elm, and hornbeam, as well as mosses and ferns. You will cross Persimmon Branch at 0.4 mile. Turn left and begin the return loop at 1 mile. From the dam, *Lake Trail* circles the lake along its edge through a picnic area and a large campground. The lake has a large variety of ducks and other waterfowl.

WILKES COUNTY

Formed in 1778, the 765-square-mile county is named for John Wilkes, an English political leader who supported American independence. The county's seat of government is Wilkesboro, through which passes US-421, a major artery between Winston-Salem and Boone.

The county leases Wilkes County Reservoir Park from the Corps of Engineers. This park offers a boat launch, picnic shelters, a beach, and a campground with 40 sites but no electricity or flush toilets. Among its paths is an unnamed 0.5-mile nature trail without signs. To reach the park, drive 6 miles west on US-421 from the junction of US-421 Business and US-421 Bypass at Wilkes Mall in Wilkesboro. Turn south on Recreation Road at the sign.

Wilkes County's Scenic Byway, a motor trail, gives access to the walking trails at W. Kerr Scott Dam and Reservoir and the Park at River's

Edge. Among the byway's attractions are a historical marker about Fort Hamby, a homestead that was reportedly once inhabited by Daniel and Rebecca Boone, and the Tom Dooley Museum, which offers an art gallery, a country store, and a Daniel Boone replica cabin. To reach the byway, take NC-268 west off US-421 Bypass.

Address: Wilkes County Parks and Recreation, 110 North Street, Wilkesboro, NC 28697 (910-651-7335 or 910-651-7305). For information on other nearby trails, see the sections on W. Kerr Scott Dam and Reservoir in chapter 1, Rendezvous Mountain Educational State Forest in chapter 2, and Wilkesboro/North Wilkesboro in chapter 4.

The Park at River's Edge

This scenic and valuable county park features an old, 1-mile airport runway that may be used for driving, biking, walking, and jogging. Between the old runway and the Yadkin River is a large, grassy plain available for baseball, softball, and soccer games. A wide gravel and rock-dust trail connects the riverside area and the old runway.

River's Edge Trail

Length and Difficulty: 2 miles, easy

Trailhead and Description: From the junction of US-421 Bypass and NC-268 (River Street), drive 0.7 mile southwest to Stokes Street and turn right near the James Wellborn historical marker and the east end of Wilkes County Industrial Park. After 0.2 mile, turn left onto the old runway. After another 0.1 mile, look for the gravel and rock-dust trail on the right. If parking here, follow the loop through the grassy field to the bank of the Yadkin River and curve left. You will follow the river in the shade of large sycamore, river birch, poplar, and walnut trees. Curve left after 1 mile to reach the old runway at 1.2 miles. Turn left on the old runway. You will pass restrooms at 1.6 miles on your return to the point of origin. Parking is also allowed at the restrooms and the west end of the old runway.

Greensboro Arboretum Trail, Greensboro

Chapter 4

TRAILS IN MUNICIPAL PARKS
AND RECREATION AREAS

More than 135 cities and towns in North Carolina have departments of parks and recreation. Some towns whose boundaries join have formed joint departments, and other cities have teamed with their counties for cooperative services. A few cities are moving swiftly with long-range master plans for greenway systems that will not only serve the inner city but connect with other cities and into the counties. An example is the Raleigh/Durham/Chapel Hill/Cary/Research Triangle greenway plan, influenced strongly by a citizens' group, the Triangle Greenways Council. Winston-Salem has a plan to connect with other towns in Forsyth County. Other communities with plans are Charlotte/Mecklenburg County and High Point/Jamestown/Greensboro/Guilford County.

According to 1994–95 figures compiled by city planning departments and chambers of commerce, Greensboro ranked third among the state's major cities with its $14.5 million parks and recreation budget; its per-resident spending of $76 ranked second. The city of Winston-Salem budgeted $7.4 million ($44 per resident).

Urban trails are usually used for walking, jogging, biking, and in-line skating. They frequently follow streams, city utility routes, nonmotorized roads, recreational parks, and historic areas. Urban trails provide opportunities for appreciating cities' heritage and culture at a relaxed pace, for meeting neighbors, and for physical and spiritual health. Urban walking clubs are growing in popularity, and books and magazines on urban trails are increasing; examples are *Walking* magazine and the book *City Safaris*, by Carolyn Shaffer.

"Trails for day use must be developed in and near urban areas," stated the National Park Service in 1986 when it was developing a national trails system plan. On the following pages are examples of diverse trails whose treadways are city soil, asphalt, brick, and cement. They lead into history and remind us that urban trails are heritage trails.

ALBEMARLE
Stanly County

The city has two trails, one in Rock Creek Park and the other in Northwoods Park.

To access Rock Creek Park, go immediately right after turning south on US-52 at the junction with NC-24/27/73. Begin *Rock Creek Trail* at the far end of the parking area. You will pass a number of park buildings, located to the right. You will follow a wide, easy, old railroad grade 1 mile to a dead end. Tall pine and hardwoods comprise a canopy over shrubs and honeysuckle. Rock Creek, to the right, partially parallels the railroad. Backtrack.

To reach Northwoods Park, take US-52 north from Rock Creek Park to US-52 Bypass at 2.2 miles. Turn right and go 1.3 miles. Turn right on Centerview Church Road, then turn left immediately. Park at the swimming pool parking lot. Begin the unnamed trail at the edge of the hardwood forest. You will follow a path for a loop of 1.5 miles in either direction. The trail ascends and descends in a hilly area, both on old woods roads and through a section with physical-fitness stations. (USGS maps: Albemarle SW and NW)

Address: Director, Parks and Recreation Department, Box 190, Albemarle, NC 28001 (704-983-3514)

BURLINGTON
Alamance County

The Burlington Recreation and Parks Department and the Burlington Women's Club sponsor Town and Country Nature Park, which offers the easy, 1.5-mile *Town and Country Nature Trail.*

Access to the park is from I-85/40 and NC-87 (exit 147); drive north on South Main Street in Graham. Turn right on NC-49, follow it to US-70 (Church Street), and turn left. Go 0.9 mile and turn right on McKinney Street. After 0.3 mile, turn right on Berkley Road; go 0.2 mile to Regent Park Lane. Park at the end of the street.

Follow the trail signs west on a well-graded path through oak, birch, Virginia pine, black willow, and wildflowers; picnic tables are located at intervals along the trail. You will cross bridges at 0.3 mile and 0.7 mile. You will pass the south side of the Haw River at 0.9 mile. Side trails go up and down the river. (USGS map: Burlington)

Address: Recreation and Parks Department, Box 1358, Burlington, NC 27215 (919-226-7371)

ELKIN
Surry County

At Elkin Municipal Park is the 0.8-mile (round-trip) *Big Elkin Nature Trail.* Access is from the northwesternmost parking area of the park. Follow the paved walking/jogging trail upstream to the West Spring Street (NC-268) bridge. Go underneath the bridge. You will pass rapids and the site of an old dam to the left at 0.3 mile. Follow the curve of the creek to a dead end near an old brick shed. Backtrack. Flora on the trail includes sycamore, walnut, cherry, rhododendron, trout lily, and blackberry.

Address and Access: Recreation and Parks Department, Box 345, Elkin, NC 28621 (910-835-9814); the address for the Foothills Nature Science Society is Box 124, Elkin, NC 28621. To access the park from I-77, exit 82, go 1.6 miles west on NC-67 to US-21. Turn right, follow US-21 for 0.7 mile to a junction on the left with West Spring Street, and go 0.8 mile to the park, on the left.

GREENSBORO
Guilford County

The city of Greensboro operates 37 parks and recreation areas. It also administers the Natural Science Center of Greensboro and a five-lake,

Bicentennial Garden Trail, Greensboro

137-acre municipal nursery at Keeley Park for the production of trees, shrubs, and flowers for the city.

The Natural Science Center has a zoo of 123 species, a planetarium, and a museum in a 30-acre complex. It is open daily. It offers the 0.6-mile *Zoo Trail* (which passes wildlife chiefly representing North and South America) and three connecting botanical trails—*Wildwood, Salamander,* and *Muskrat Trails*—which total 0.3 mile. Bioluminescent mush-

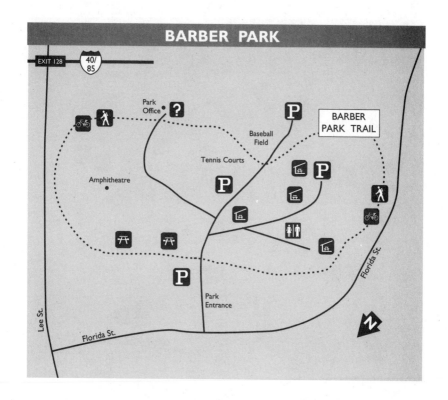

BARBER PARK

EXIT 128 · 40/85

Park Office

? · BARBER PARK TRAIL

Baseball Field

Tennis Courts

P

Amphitheatre

P

P

P

P

Park Entrance

Lee St.

Florida St.

Florida St.

N

rooms grow on a bank near a stream. The center is located at 4310 Lawndale Drive, 2.5 miles north of the junction of Lawndale and US-220 (Battleground Avenue) in the northwest part of the city. For information, call 910-288-3769. The Natural Science Center adjoins Country Park, described below.

The city has a 50-mile labyrinth of bicycle trails, some of which are also used for hiking, birding, skating, and jogging. A number of parks have unnamed paths and others only physical-fitness courses. Some areas, such as Hamilton Lake, have a path nearby. The 0.9-mile *Hamilton Lake Trail* begins at the corner of Starmount Drive and East Keeling Road at Lake Hamilton. It follows right of Starmount Drive on pea gravel through an open forest of tall and magnificent hickory, oak, poplar, pine, and beech. An excellent trail for viewing autumn foliage, it ends at the corner of Kemp Road and Starmount.

Barber Park is an ultramodern and spaciously landscaped facility featuring the Indoor Sports Pavilion dome for tennis and volleyball. It offers sheltered picnic platforms, athletic fields, and the remark-

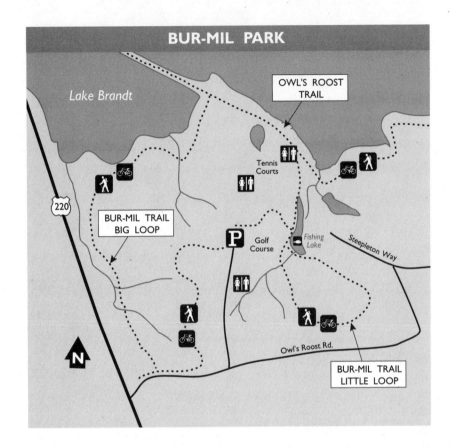

able, 1-mile *Barber Park Trail*. This cement loop is designed for the physically disabled. It passes through the forest on the northwest side and sweeps around a grassy area elsewhere. Wild rose, cow-itch vine, wild grapevine, and honeysuckle garnish the eastern fence line. Access is off I-40, exit 128. Drive west on East Lee Street to Florida Street. Turn left to the park entrance, on the left.

Bur-Mil Park is an expansive and popular facility of 247 acres on the northwestern edge of the city. The park is off US-220 at 5834 Owl's Roost Road East; the entrance is on the left (north). Bur-Mil Park is bordered on the north partly by Lake Brandt and Brush Creek and on the northwest by Lake Higgins. Its facilities include swimming pools, golf courses, tennis courts, two fishing ponds, picnic shelters, athletic fields, volleyball courts, a playground, a clubhouse, a restaurant, and two multiple-use trails. The trails are connected by a 0.4-mile section of *Owl's Roost Trail* (see the Greensboro Watershed Trails section below). The park's 2-

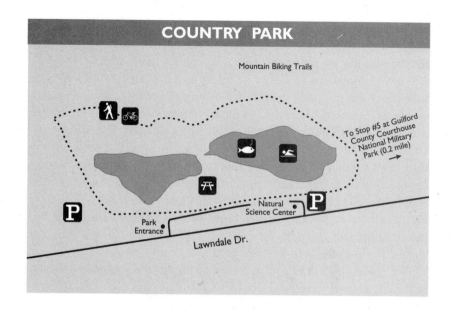

Mountain Biking Trails

To Stop #5 at Guilford County Courthouse National Military Park (0.2 mile) →

Natural Science Center

Park Entrance

Lawndale Dr.

mile *Big Loop Trail* makes a circuit on the west side of the park. The most convenient access is at picnic shelter #1 at a parking lot off Owl's Roost Road; bear left before the park entrance road. Follow the trail through a forest of tall poplar, pine, sweet gum, and running cedar. You will cross a number of bridges over small streams, the last of which is 0.2 mile before a junction with *Owl's Roost Trail*. (To the left on *Owl's Roost Trail* is a bridge over a narrow part of the lake.) Turn right and follow the trail to a pier on the left and access to a parking lot on the right near picnic shelter #6. Follow the gravel road past the shelter to the swimming pool and picnic shelter #3 to complete the loop, or continue on *Owl's Roost Trail* for 0.1 mile to a fork on the right and a junction with the 1-mile *Little Loop Trail*. Follow it around Fishing Lake; you will reach the clubhouse by picnic shelter #7. To complete *Big Loop Trail*, follow it south from picnic shelter #3 to the point of origin. The park's phone number is 910-545-5300.

Country Park, also in the northwestern part of the city, adjoins the Natural Science Center on the northwest (only 110 yards separate the two facilities' parking lots), Lewis Recreation Center on the south, and Guilford Courthouse National Military Park on the north. Access is off US-220. Turn right on Pisgah Church Road, go four blocks, and turn left on Lawndale Drive North. Turn left on Nathanael Greene Drive to reach the parking area and office. The facilities include a lake for fishing, picnic shelters, volleyball courts, rental boats, and a special 0.5-mile trail for the visually impaired. Another trail, the 1.6-mile *Country Park Trail*, is a paved loop around the park. There is a 0.2-mile connector bike/hike trail from the parking lot north to stop #5 on the bike/hike trail in Guilford Courthouse National Military Park. There is also a trail for mountain bikes. One of the city's oldest parks, Country Park dates from 1924. It has an impressive history. Some of its special events are the Carolina Cup Bicycle Road Race, one of the largest cycling events in the United States; the December Candlefest, which involves 2,500 Girl Scouts; the Wild Turkey Fat Tire Festival, a mountain-bike race; and the Farmers' Market, which features vegetables and homemade crafts. For information, call the park office at 910-545-5342 or 910-545-5343. For shelter reservations, call 910-545-5300.

Oka T. Hester Park is a more recent facility in the southwestern part of the city east of Sedgefield Country Club. The park offers a large center for community activities, a lake with paddleboats, a picnic area, a playground, tennis and volleyball courts, and a physical-fitness trail. The 1.3-mile *Hester Park Trail* loops around the beautiful lake. From I-40 and US-29A/70A, exit 217, go 1.8 miles west on US-29A/70A to Groometown Road and turn left. After 0.9 mile, turn left to Ailanthus Street and Oka T. Hester Park.

Lake Daniel Park has an easy, 3.5-mile asphalt biking, hiking, and exercise trail that runs between the park complex and Latham Park. On *Lake Daniel Trail*, the mileage is marked. Entry can be made at a number of streets between the points of origin. To walk the distance given above, begin on Lake Drive near Battleground Avenue and proceed west (near an eastward-flowing stream) to North Elam Avenue near Wesley Long Community Hospital. The meadows are open and grassy, with scattered oak, ash, poplar, and pine. Using a city bike map is advisable at this park.

Working with Guilford County, the city has an expansive long-range plan for greenways and bike/hike trails that will encompass the entire county. The bike trails currently within the city proper will have at least 10 new access routes to connect with *Mountains-to-Sea Bike Route #2*, which passes through the south side of the county. When completed, the outstanding *Bicentennial Greenway Trail* will be the longest trail in the state to connect multiple cities. Currently, a 6.2-mile greenway section runs from High Point Lake at High Point/Jamestown north to Regency Road near I-40 (see the information on High Point in this chapter). The northern section will cross I-40, pass east of Piedmont Triad International Airport, go northeast near Horsepen Creek, turn east, turn southeast along Old Battlefield Road, and junction with existing greenways at Guilford Courthouse National Military Park. From there, it will connect with Jaycee Park and Country Park. The master plan shows the potential for the route north to connect with the lake system of trails, including the *Mountains-to-Sea Trail*.

Address: Parks and Recreation Department, Box 3136, Greensboro, NC 27402 (910-373-2574)

Gardens of Greensboro

The city has three major gardens: Bicentennial Garden, the Greensboro Arboretum, and Bog Garden. All are in the heart of the city within a few blocks of, or adjoining, each other. These day-use gardens are open all year. Admission is free. The gardens are made possible by a partnership of the Greensboro Parks and Recreation Department and Greensboro Beautiful, a nonprofit, volunteer organization affiliated with Keep America Beautiful. Brochures as elegant as the gardens themselves are available on location. Visits to these parks lift the human spirit. The poetic expressions on one of the brochures are inspiring: "I want to surround myself with the symmetry of nature, rejoice in its beauty. . . . I'm feeling a little wild with boundaries undefined. . . . The world is wide and bright and wonderful. . . . I can indulge exotic fantasies of faraway places."

Address: Greensboro Beautiful, Inc., Box 3136, Greensboro, NC 27402 (910-373-2558 or 800-344-2282)

The Greensboro Arboretum is located within Lindley Park, which may be accessed off West Market Street by driving south on Green Valley Road, then immediately going right on one-way Starmount Drive to a parking area. From the end of the parking area (near a basketball court), walk to an arched bridge over a stream. You can make a 1.3-mile loop on *Greensboro Arboretum Trail*, but the distance is longer if you use spur trails for a closer examination of the collection areas and go off the trail to the dancing fountain. Hundreds of species in the collections of conifers, sun shrubs, wildflowers, small trees, hydrophytic plants, vines, shade shrubs, and ground covers make this an alluring horticultural delight. Birds and butterflies are prominent visitors.

GARDENS OF GREENSBORO

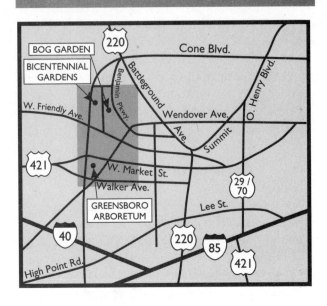

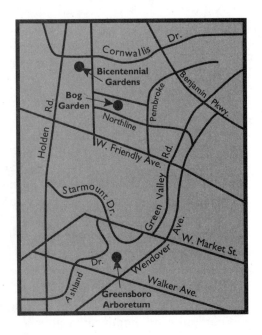

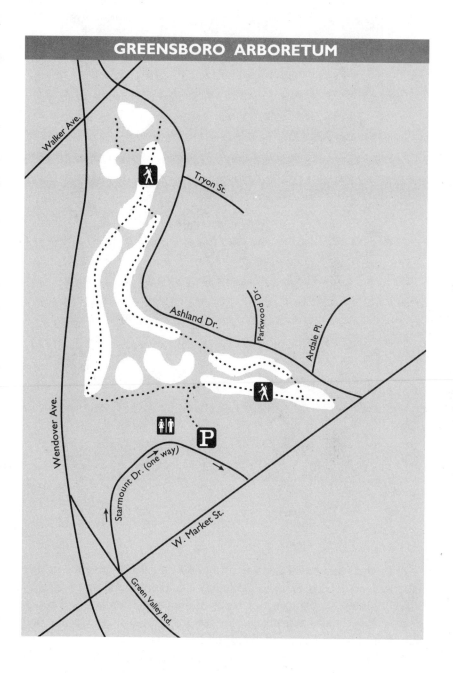

Trail marker in Hagan-Stone Park, Greensboro

To locate Bicentennial Garden, turn north off Friendly Avenue to 1105 Hobbs Road. The park is meticulously maintained and specializes in mass regimented plantings of bulbs, annuals, perennials, and roses. Follow the 0.5-mile *Bicentennial Garden Trail* to a bridge over a small stream and into a lightly wooded garden where more than 100 plants are located in a fragrance garden and an herb garden; the labels include a Braille version. The area is part of Caldwell Memorial Park, named in honor of David Caldwell (1725–1824), patriot, statesman, clergyman, physician, and founder of Caldwell Log College in 1767.

Near Bicentennial Garden is Bog Garden, located east of Hobbs Road between Starmount Farm Road (to the north) and Northline Avenue (to the south); Pembroke Road is to the east. Bog Garden features aquatic plants such as cattail, iris, lily, sedge, and arum, which need wet, spongy, acidic soil. Additionally, the bog entices duck, goose, and heron. The paved *Bog Garden Trail*, usable by visitors with wheelchairs, runs around the lake. There are boardwalks and a hillside path.

Hagan-Stone Park

In 1964, Greensboro established a scenic 409-acre regional park near the town of Pleasant Garden. It is named in honor of Anne Hagan and Joseph J. Stone, leaders in land conservation and natural resources in the Greensboro area. Developed from forests, farms, and fields, Hagan-Stone Park has a full-service tent/RV campground, a primitive campground, and a group campground. It offers six picnic shelters; three playgrounds; softball fields; volleyball courts; four lakes stocked with bluegill, largemouth bass, and shellcracker; canoe and paddleboat rentals; and a 5K-8K cross-country course that accommodates state and regional high-school and collegiate meets.

In addition, the park offers Camp Joy (where there is a swimming pool) and a rental day-camp facility for children and adults with special disabilities. Within the main park area is the reconstructed Oak Grove School House, which serves as a learning center for local elementary and middle-school teachers and students. The park's hiking trails are described below. (USGS map: Climax)

Address and Access: Hagan-Stone Park, 5920 Hagan-Stone Park Road, Pleasant Garden, NC 27313 (910-674-0472, office; 910-373-5888, shelter reservations; 910-674-3571, Camp Joy, summer only). From the junction of I-40/85 and US-421 in Greensboro, go south on US-421 for 6.6 miles, turn right on Hagan-Stone Park Road (SR-3411), and go 2.3 miles to the park entrance, on the right. From the junction of US-421 and NC-62 near Julian, go north on US-421 for 4.1 miles and turn left.

Louise Chatfield Hiking Trail *(3.4 miles)*
Dogwood Trail *(0.5 mile)*
Harold Draper Nature Trail *(1.5 miles)*
Schoolhouse Trail *(0.3 mile)*
Ridge Trail *(0.8 mile)*

Length and Difficulty: 6.5 miles combined round-trip, easy

Trailheads and Description: After entering the park, turn left to a parking area near the trail center. Descend to the lake and begin the trails clockwise.

The red-signed *Louise Chatfield Hiking Trail* connects with all the other trails. If following this trail, you will enter an old forest road that is also the blue-signed *Dogwood Trail* and part of the circle of the yellow-signed *Harold Draper Nature Trail*. After 0.1 mile in a hardwood forest, turn off the old road on a foot trail. You will descend to cross a small bridge and go upstream to a junction where *Dogwood Trail* turns right at 0.3 mile. (*Dogwood Trail* crosses a footbridge over a small stream and ascends in a rocky area for 0.1 mile to junction with *Harold Draper Nature Trail*, right and left. If you turn right, you will descend near a parking area, a picnic shelter, and lake #2; you will then cross a stream at the upper edge of the lake and follow a forest road back to the trail center.)

Continuing on *Louise Chatfield Hiking Trail* and *Harold Draper Nature Trail*, you will ascend slightly in a rocky area to pass left of the primitive tent and group campgrounds. At 0.7 mile, *Louise Chatfield Hiking Trail* turns left at a signpost and *Harold Draper Nature Trail* turns right. (A return can be made here on *Harold Draper Nature Trail*. After a few feet, you will pass a memory bench placed by the T. Gilbert Pearson Audubon Society in honor of Draper, who lived from 1914 to 1995. You will then cross an old forest road and gently descend to cross a footbridge at 0.2 mile. At 0.3 mile, you will curve right at the headwaters of lake #4, enter a grassy field, and pass left of the RV campground and right of a restored tobacco barn. You will see connecting routes of the 8K cross-country route in this area. At 0.55 mile, you will cross the campground road and connect with *Dogwood Trail*, right and left. Stay left to return to the trail center.)

After leaving *Harold Draper Nature Trail*, *Louise Chatfield Hiking Trail* curves east and reaches the Oak Grove School House at 1.3 miles. (Here, the short *Schoolhouse Trail* loops to connect with a softball field and pic-

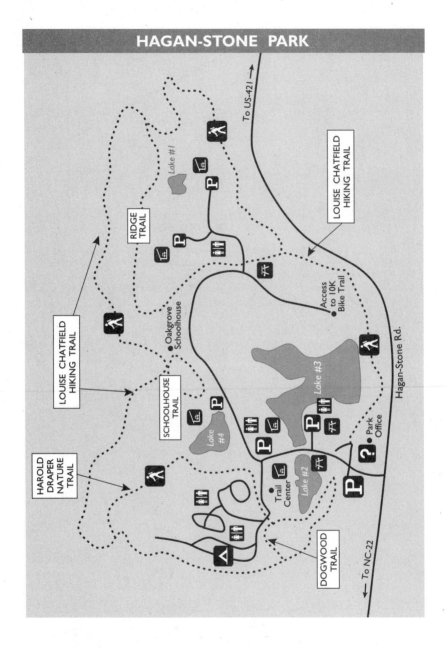

To US-421 →

LOUISE CHATFIELD HIKING TRAIL

Lake #1

RIDGE TRAIL

LOUISE CHATFIELD HIKING TRAIL

Oakgrove Schoolhouse

SCHOOLHOUSE TRAIL

HAROLD DRAPER NATURE TRAIL

Access to 10K Bike Trail

Hagan-Stone Rd.

Lake #3

Lake #4

Lake #2

Park Office

Trail Center

DOGWOOD TRAIL

→ To NC-22

nic shelter #4.) On *Louise Chatfield Hiking Trail*, you will soon enter an open field with yellow pine and cedar borders, pass a 5K-8K route on the right that leads to *Ridge Trail*, and junction with the orange-signed

GREENSBORO WATERSHED TRAILS

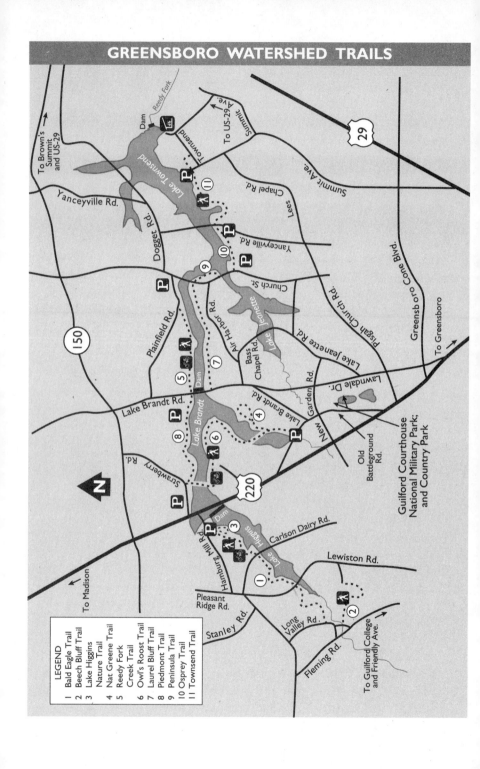

LEGEND

1 Bald Eagle Trail
2 Beech Bluff Trail
3 Lake Higgins Nature Trail
4 Nat Greene Trail
5 Reedy Fork Creek Trail
6 Owl's Roost Trail
7 Laurel Bluff Trail
8 Piedmont Trail
9 Peninsula Trail
10 Osprey Trail
11 Townsend Trail

Ridge Trail at 2 miles. (*Ridge Trail* passes to the right of lake #1 and follows an old, straight fence lined with cedar and pine. At 0.4 mile, you will reach an intersection with a 5K-8K route; go straight ahead. At 0.7 mile, you will junction with an access leading left to restrooms and picnic shelter #5; to the right, a service road goes to a park road. You will cross a gravel road, pass left of a tennis court, and junction with *Louise Chatfield Hiking Trail* at 0.8 mile.)

Continuing on *Louise Chatfield Hiking Trail* at the first junction, you will pass through groves of dogwood and by an open field to the right. You will also pass twice under a power line. You will then enter a pine forest. At 2.7 miles, you will reach a junction with *Ridge Trail* to the right (the second junction). Continue ahead through locust, cedar, and oak. At 3 miles, you will junction with a service-road access (right) to a park road cul-de-sac. You will then pass left of lake #3 to reach the park office. Across the entrance road is the trail center parking lot; you will complete the loop at 3.4 miles.

Greensboro Watershed Trails

Lake Brandt

Lake Brandt, located between Lake Higgins and Lake Townsend, is one of the city's watershed lakes. It has a marina on the south side that offers fishing and boating but no swimming. Cooperative efforts among the city, the county, and private citizens have created and maintain the five hiking trails at Lake Brandt and the two at Lake Townsend. At Lake Higgins Marina is the 0.4-mile *Nature Trail*. It begins near the boat ramp, partially follows the lake, and loops through hardwoods, Virginia pine, sparkleberry, and club moss. Access is 0.4 mile off US-220 on Hamburg Mill Road (0.9 mile north of the Bur-Mil Park entrance on US-220). (USGS maps: Lake Brandt, Summerfield)

Address and Access: Lake Brandt Marina, 5945 Lake Brandt Road, Greensboro, NC 27455 (910-545-5333). From the northwestern section of the city at the junction of US-220 (Battleground Avenue) and Lawndale Drive, follow Lawndale Drive (which becomes Lake Brandt Road) 5.3 miles north to the dam. Park in the roadside space.

Nat Greene Trail (*3.5 miles*)
Owl's Roost Trail (*4.4 miles*)
Piedmont Trail (*2.8 miles*)
Reedy Fork Creek Trail (*3.7 miles*)
Laurel Bluff Trail (*3.3 miles*)

Length and Difficulty: 17.7 miles combined, easy

Connecting Trails: Big Loop Trail, Peninsula Trail

Trailheads and Description: At the dam, hike south on the road for 0.1 mile to enter the forest (right) on *Nat Greene Trail*. This state trail honors Nathanael Greene, who led the colonial army against Lord Cornwallis at Guilford Courthouse on March 15, 1781; Greene is the man for whom the city is named. You will pass the parking area of Lake Brandt Marina at 0.2 mile in a forest of poplar, beech, and Virginia pine. You will then weave in and out of coves for periodic views of the lake, cross a small stream at 1.6 miles, and junction with *Owl's Roost Trail* (right) on an old railroad grade at 2.8 miles. Cross the old railroad grade. After 0.2 mile, you will enter a marsh. You will cross a wide, 225-foot-long boardwalk at 3.4 miles and pass through a floodplain to Old Battlefield Road at 3.5 miles, the end of the trail. (To the right, it is 0.7 mile to US-220.)

To continue the loop, backtrack to *Owl's Roost Trail* and follow it north on the old railroad grade. You will cross a railroad bridge at 0.3 mile and exit the railroad grade to the right into a pine grove. After a few yards, you will enter a forest of oak, hickory, ironwood, tag alder, running cedar, and scattered rattlesnake orchid. You will cross a small stream at 1 mile and reach an excellent view of the dam and marina across the lake at 1.6 miles. At 3.1 miles, you will enter a boggy area. You will rejoin the old railroad grade at 3.5 miles, pass through the northeast corner of Bur-Mil Park at *Big Loop Trail*, and cross a 295-foot railroad bridge at 3.8 miles; traffic can be seen to the left on US-220. You will enter a pastoral area at 4 miles and reach a junction with *Piedmont Trail* (right) at 4.2 miles. Continue ahead for 0.2 mile to a junction with Strawberry Road (SR-2321) and a small parking area. (To the left, it is 0.2 mile to US-220.)

Backtrack to *Piedmont Trail*, on the left. You will enter a grazing field featuring cedar, honeysuckle, wild plum, and blackberry. At 0.5 mile, you will descend into a seepage area at the base of a farm pond and the lake's edge. You will then enter another open area and cross a small stream at 1 mile and at 1.2 miles. You will cross a boardwalk at 1.6 miles and a bridge over a stream at 2.6 miles before reaching Lake Brandt Road (SR-2347) at 2.8 miles. (To the right, it is 0.3 mile across the bridge to a parking area for *Nat Greene Trail*.)

Begin *Reedy Fork Creek Trail* across the road from *Piedmont Trail*. You will enter a forest of oak, river birch, sycamore, and sweet gum and head downstream. You will cross a gas pipeline at 0.5 mile, then cross a stream on a footbridge built by Boy Scout Troop 275, then enter a laurel grove. At 1.3 miles, turn sharply left from Reedy Creek (the backwater of Lake Townsend). To the right, you will briefly join an old woods road at 2.1 miles. You will pass through wildflowers such as fire pink, black cohosh, bloodroot, wild geranium, and buttonbush before arriving at Hendricks Road (SR-2324) at 3.2 miles near the guardrail. Turn right on the road and cross a scenic marsh causeway frequented by waterfowl. At 3.7 miles, you will reach a junction with Church Street (SR-1001). (To the right, it is 6.4 miles on Church Street and west on Pisgah Church Road to US-220.) Turn right and cross the bridge over the lake. After 0.1 mile, you will reach a junction to the right with *Laurel Bluff Trail*. (To the left across the road is the northern trailhead of *Peninsula Trail* at Lake Townsend, described below.)

Laurel Bluff Trail runs through the Roger Jones Bird Sanctuary. It enters a river-birch grove at 0.1 mile. You will follow an old woods road for a short distance and pass the boundary of a field at 1.6 miles. Among the trees are willow oak, shagbark hickory, black gum, maple, and poplar. The shrubs and wildflowers include wood betony, beauty-bush, arum, laurel, redbud, dogwood, and filbert. You will cross a small brook near the edge of the lake at 2 miles and reach a boggy area at 2.1 miles. Bear right at a fork at 2.3 miles. You will pass a spur trail to the left at 2.7 miles. You will then pass through a large beech grove at 2.8 miles, cross a gas pipeline at 3.1 miles, pass an old barn, and reach the former Dillard's Store on Lake Brandt Road at 3.3 miles. To the left across the road is *Nat Greene Trail*.

Lake Higgins

Lake Higgins is the product of a dam on Brush Creek northwest of Greensboro. The dam is near the west side of US-220, and its outlet is under the highway, from which point the waters flow east to join Reedy Creek on the way into Lake Brandt. From there, the waters flow into Lake Townsend under Church Street Extension. Lake Higgins has a marina for boating and fishing and is open daily. To access the lake, go

0.4 mile off US-220 on Hamburg Mill Road, located 0.9 mile north of the Bur-Mil Park entrance on US-220. (USGS maps: Summerfield, Lake Brandt)

Lake Higgins Nature Trail *(0.4 mile)*
Bald Eagle Trail *(4 miles)*
Beech Bluff Trail *(1 mile)*

Length and Difficulty: 5.4 miles combined, easy

Trailhead and Description: The trailhead for *Lake Higgins Nature Trail* is at the southwest corner of the marina parking area near the boat ramp. The trail partially follows the lake, then loops through hardwoods, Virginia pine, sparkleberry, and club moss for a return to the parking area.

Access to *Bald Eagle Trail* is on Hamburg Mill Road just beyond the Lake Higgins Marina entrance sign. A gravel parking area is located here. This narrow, white-blazed trail is sponsored by the Greensboro Fat Tire Society. A multiuse route for mountain bikers and hikers, it is predominantly used by mountain bikers. Paralleling the lakeshore, the trail stays in the young forest enough to prevent bikers and hikers from seeing much of the lake except in the wintertime. Occasionally, the path ripples over old tobacco rows from past farmland. Generally a flat treadway, the route passes through a forest of Virginia pine, Eastern red cedar, sourwood, dogwood, and sweet gum. Yellow poplar, hickory, and American elm are in a few coves. There are patches of club moss, periwinkle, poison ivy, and trumpet vine. Deer, raccoon, and squirrel inhabit the woods, and owl call each other both in the daytime and nighttime. Bald eagles have reportedly been seen in the area.

You will cross a small stream at 0.3 mile and pass through a cedar grove and across a damp area with a streamlet at 1 mile and 1.1 miles. At 1.2 miles is an embankment on which grows pinxter. You will cross Carlson Dairy Road at 1.6 miles. (To the right, it is 0.7 mile to a Texaco service station and a junction with Pleasant Ridge Road.) At 1.9 miles are a damp area and a small stream, followed by two switchbacks up a slight incline and two switchbacks down. You will cross a natural-gas pipeline at 2.4 miles, then enter a damp and flat area among alder; to the right, private homes can be seen through the trees. You will cross a paved road at 2.9 miles.

After a grove of Virginia pine are two small streamlets that may be dry in summer. You will see the edge of an old field to the right at 3.2 miles. You will cross a sewage line at 3.6 miles, then have views of a farm field to the right. After a small stream, you will ascend an embankment near a large beech tree. To the left is a swampy area near Brush Creek. You will reach the gravel Long Valley Road at 4 miles; there is no parking here. To the left, it is 110 yards to the gravel Brass Eagle Loop Road. To the right, it is 0.9 mile to Pleasant Ridge Road, where a right turn leads 2.1 miles to Hamburg Mill Road and the Lake Higgins Marina trailhead.

To reach *Beech Bluff Trail* from the southwestern trailhead of *Bald Eagle Trail*, turn left on Brass Eagle Loop Road to cross the bridge over Brush Creek. Go 270 feet on the gravel Brass Eagle Loop Road to the white-blazed trail, located on the left; there is no parking here. For the first 0.2 mile, the deep forest features tall yellow poplar and ash holding large, ropelike wild grapevine. The narrow and rarely used path ascends a hillside for scenic views of the Brush Creek forest and wildfowl. Black cohosh, Christmas fern, and dwarf iris are on the hillside. Large beech and oak are prominent. At 0.5 mile, you will descend to cross a sewage line, then cross a gully (which may have water), then enter a floodplain area. You will pass under large trees, pass a utilities maintenance area, and follow a service road to Lewiston Road at 1 mile. Backtrack.

If accessing either *Bald Eagle Trail* or *Beech Bluff Trail* from the southwestern trailheads, one route from I-40 is to take exit 215 and follow Guilford College Road north for 2.2 miles to West Friendly Avenue. Turn left, then quickly right on New Garden Road, which will take you past Guilford College for 0.8 mile to Fleming Road. Follow Fleming Road 3.5 miles to Brass Eagle Loop Road, on the right. It is 0.2 mile to *Beach Bluff Trail*, on the right.

Lake Townsend

Lake Townsend is fed by Lake Higgins, Lake Brandt, and Richard Lake. All the waters flow east. At the east end of Lake Townsend is its dam. Adjoining the lake/dam area is Bryan Park, one of the city's largest. Bryan Park is known for its golf courses. Three Lake Townsend–area trails are described below.

Peninsula Trail *(1.2 miles)*
Osprey Trail *(2.5 miles)*
Townsend Trail *(4.2 miles)*

Length and Difficulty: 7.9 miles combined, easy

Connecting Trail: Laurel Bluff Trail

Trailheads and Description: From the junction of Pisgah Church Road (its northeast end, where it becomes Lees Chapel Road) and Church Street, go 2 miles north to a roadside parking area on the right for *Osprey Trail,* also on the right. Ahead, across the causeway, it is 1 mile to the northern trailhead of *Peninsula Trail.* To the left across the road is the trailhead for *Laurel Bluff Trail.* To reach the eastern trailhead of *Osprey Trail,* go 2.1 miles north on Yanceyville Road from Lees Chapel Road. Here also is the western trailhead of *Townsend Trail;* its eastern trailhead is accessed by taking Lees Chapel Road northeast to the junction of Southshore Road and Townsend Road.

Enter the white-blazed *Peninsula Trail* through young Virginia pine. At 0.6 mile is a spot for observing Lake Townsend. After a wet runoff area is a mixed pine and magnolia grove at 0.9 mile. Exit at North Church Road at 1.2 miles, turn left, and cross the causeway for 300 yards to a roadside parking area on the left (east). *Osprey Trail* begins here. Follow the white-blazed trail past the remains of an old cabin at 0.2 mile. At 0.3 mile, you will pass close to the lake's lapping shoreline. You will ascend a slight ridge of oak and pine and descend to parallel a cove before rock-hopping a stream at 0.8 mile. You will return to the lake's edge, then cross under two power lines to follow a rim of a former pond. At 2.1 miles is an excellent view of the lake. You will arrive at Yanceyville Road at 2.5 miles. Backtrack, or have a second vehicle waiting for you. It is 5.9 miles on the roads back to the point of origin.

The white-blazed *Townsend Trail* begins across the road at a gate opposite *Osprey Trail.* You will pass through a grassy slope by the lake for about 110 yards and enter the forest at a berm. On the left at 0.4 mile is an old well in a forest of oak, beech, and dogwood. You will curve around a long cove, cross a stream, and return to the lakeside at 1 mile. At 1.6 miles, you will walk on the sandy edge of the lake to avoid dense growth under a power line. Here are buttonbush, filbert, and tag alder. Reenter the forest and follow the edge of another cove. You will cross a footbridge and enter a grove of Virginia pine and club moss. Ridges on the treadway at 2.7 miles indicate a former tobacco field. You will pass under a power line at 3.1 miles and 3.4 miles, then curve right of a farm pond and ascend at 3.7 miles. At 3.8 miles, you will cross Southshore Road to reenter the woods, then exit to a field with bluebird houses in Bryan Park. Cross the field and turn right at a fence. After a few yards, you will enter the fence opening and arrive at the paved Townsend Road at 4.2 miles. To the left are Bryan Park's golf courses. Turn right, go 0.2 mile on the road to a park gate, and exit at the corner of Southshore Road and Townsend Road by the railroad track. Backtrack, or have a second vehicle parked at the open space outside the gate between Townsend Road and the railroad, to avoid being locked inside the park. (USGS maps: Lake Brandt, Browns Summit)

HIGH POINT
Guilford County

High Point is following the trend of fellow Triad cities Greensboro and Winston-Salem in its long-range plans for a greenway system. At present, a 1.4-mile section of *Boulding Branch Trail* is completed. To access its southwestern trailhead, go east off North Main Street on Farris Avenue to its junction with Forest Street. You will follow an asphalt trail downstream and go through a cement tunnel at Centennial Street at 0.2 mile. You will then pass through the High Point University campus between West College Drive and East College Drive at 0.5 mile and 0.6 mile. At 1.2 miles, you will reach East Lexington Avenue. To the left is High Point Museum and Historic Park. Ahead and to the right of the trail is the Little Red Schoolhouse, built in 1930 as Ray Street Elementary School downtown and moved here in 1987. At 1.3 miles, you may access Welborn Middle School by going west across a footbridge. Continue to the right on the main trail and exit at the junction of Woodruff and Wiltshire Streets. When the remaining 3 miles of the trail are completed downstream to Deep River and connect with *Bicentennial Greenway Trail* at Penny Road, High Point and Jamestown will be joined by a greenway system.

The city also contributes about 65 percent of the funding for Piedmont Environmental Center, a 200-acre preserve for natural-science

Boulding Branch Trail, High Point

study at High Point City Lake. One of its services is an outdoor class-room program for public schoolchildren. The center also has a special wildflower garden that emphasizes plants from the Piedmont. Picnick-ing is allowed, but camping and swimming are not. The center is open daily.

Address and Access: Parks and Recreation Department, 221 Nathan Hunt Drive, High Point, NC 27260 (910-887-3477). The address for Pied-mont Environmental Center is 1228 Penny Road, High Point, NC 27260 (910-883-8531). To reach the environmental center from the junction of US-29A/70A and Penny Road west of Jamestown, go north for 1.1 miles on Penny Road and turn right at the center's entrance. From the junc-tion of Wendover Avenue and I-40, exit 214, in Greensboro, go south-west on Wendover for 4.5 miles to the junction with Penny Road at the Deep River intersection. Turn left and go 2 miles to the center, on the left.

Piedmont Environmental Center

Lakeshore Trail *(1.8 miles)*
Fence Row Trail *(0.1 mile)*
Wildflower Trail *(0.2 mile)*
Fiddlehead Trail *(0.4 mile)*
Dogwood Trail *(0.6 mile)*
Pine Thicket Trail *(0.3 mile)*
Raccoon Run Trail *(0.7 mile)*
Chickadee Trail *(0.1 mile)*

Length and Difficulty: 4.2 miles combined round-trip, easy

Trailheads and Description: All the trails can be accessed from the white-blazed *Lakeshore Trail*, which begins at the parking lot or the back porch of the center. If beginning from the parking lot, you will enter at the south side near the driveway entrance and the crossing of *Bicentennial Greenway Trail*. You will immediately reach a connector to the tan-blazed *Fence Row Trail* (left) and the green-blazed *Chickadee Trail* (right); each connects with *Lakeshore Trail* after 0.1 mile. If going left, you will pass behind the parking lot and buildings, then turn right and junction with the purple-blazed *Wildflower Trail* after a few yards. (*Wildflower Trail* has double loops, connects with *Bicentennial Greenway Trail*, and passes through a mixed forest of pine, hardwoods, ferns, and wildflowers.)

Continuing on *Lakeshore Trail*, you will reach a junction with the yellow-blazed, 0.4-mile *Fiddlehead Trail* to the right. (*Fiddlehead Trail* descends to a junction with the red-blazed *Pine Thicket Trail* to the left and a cove in High Point City Lake. Here is a junction, right and left, with *Lakeshore Trail*. A right turn on the floating bridge leads back to the parking lot, for a 1-mile loop.) If you will not be hiking *Fiddlehead Trail*, go past a spur connector leading left to *Bicentennial Greenway Trail*, followed by a junction to the right with the orange-blazed *Dogwood Trail*. (*Dogwood Trail* goes through the heart of the *Lakeshore Trail* loop among oak, pine, poplar, and cedar. Along the way, it has a junction to the right with *Pine Thicket Trail*.)

Staying on *Lakeshore Trail*, you will pass through a forest of large trees and arrive at the lake at 0.8 mile. Curve around the peninsulas; the interior of the loop is kudzu. You will pass a junction with *Dogwood*

PIEDMONT ENVIRONMENTAL CENTER

BICENTENNIAL
GREENWAY TRAIL

WILDFLOWER
TRAIL

LAKESHORE TRAIL

DOGWOOD TRAIL

PINE
THICKET
TRAIL

FIDDLEHEAD
TRAIL

CHICKADEE
TRAIL

LAKESHORE TRAIL

Penny Road

High Point
City Lake

RACCOON
RUN TRAIL

Trail (right) at 1 mile and a junction with the blue-blazed *Raccoon Run Trail* (left) at 1.3 miles. (*Raccoon Run Trail* goes briefly on a linear route before making a scenic circle on the peninsula.) Finish *Lakeshore Trail* by crossing the floating bridge and ascending to the parking lot at 1.8 miles.

Three miles of *Bicentennial Greenway Trail* are within the center's preserve; see below. (USGS maps: High Point E, Guilford)

Bicentennial Greenway Trail

Length and Difficulty: 6.2 miles, easy to moderate

Connecting Trails: Twin Pond Trail (0.6 mile, easy); *Deep River Hiking Trail* (3 miles, easy); *Hollis Rogers Pinewoods Trail* (0.4 mile, easy); Piedmont Environmental Center trails

Trailhead and Description: The northern access is off I-40, exit 210. Follow NC-68 south for 0.4 mile. Turn left (east) on Regency Drive and park on the right; note that this area may become another street. Walk 290 yards farther on Regency Drive to the trailhead, located on the right (south). The southern trailhead is at the northern end of the Deep River bridge on Penny Road; parking is available 0.35 mile north on Penny Road at Piedmont Environmental Center.

Throughout the trail are tall mixed hardwoods: oak, yellow poplar, sycamore, and river birch. Virginia pine and loblolly pine thrive on the slopes. The grassy trail shoulders are frequently mowed, and the width of the landscape allows a flow of breezes. Wild rose, muscadine grape, blackberry, and August olive are prominent. Ferns and wildflowers border the woods' edges. This multiuse trail is open for bikers, pedestrians, skaters, and joggers. Horse traffic and motorized vehicles are not allowed; neither is camping. Dogs must be on a leash. Some sections are suitable for the physically handicapped.

If beginning at Regency Drive at Piedmont Centre Office Park, follow the signs on a wide asphalt trail. After negotiating steps and a boardwalk in a forest, you will arrive at a meadow of blackberry and honeysuckle. At 0.6 mile is a parking area; a sign indicates that the first 2.8 miles of the trail opened in November 1989. Continue along the East Fork of Deep River, occasionally crossing it on cement bridges. You will cross a bridge over a stream from Davis Lake (right) at 1.1 miles. At 1.3 miles is a small cascade to the left. You will cross West Wendover Avenue at 2 miles. (The access is under construction, and the trail may go under the road beside the river.)

At 2.5 miles, you will pass through Gibson Park. To the right are Deep River Cabin (built around 1830), restrooms, and an access on

Bicentennial Greenway Trail, High Point

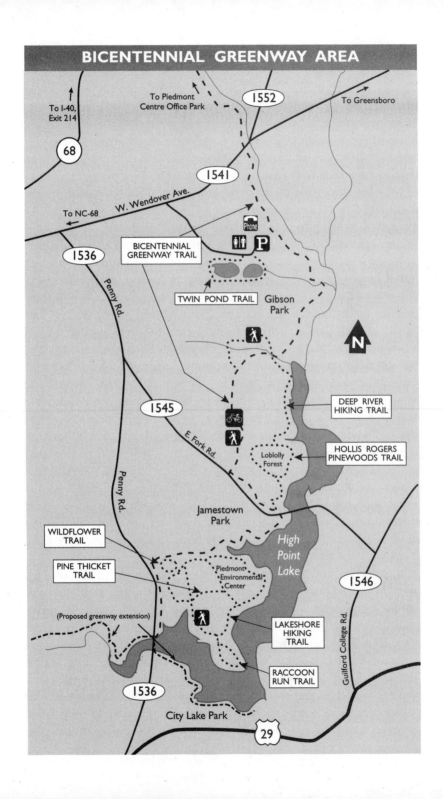

Park Entrance Road to West Wendover Avenue. On the trail is a plaque honoring the history and craftsmanship of the Jamestown Long Rifles. (To hike *Twin Pond Trail*, cross the parking area from the restrooms to the first pond on the left. Cross the dam and turn right among hardwoods, buttonbush, cattail, sensitive fern, and cardinal flower. Follow the lake border around the second pond and exit at the entrance road to the park. Turn right and return to the parking area to continue *Bicentennial Greenway Trail*. For highway access to Gibson Park from Penny Road off NC-68, follow West Wendover east for 0.9 mile to the park entrance, on the right. It is 0.3 mile to the parking lot. From I-40, exit 214, it is 3.6 miles west on Wendover to the park entrance, on the left.)

One of the most scenic areas of the trail is at 3 miles, where an observation deck juts into a swamp, providing an excellent retreat for birders. Cattail, arrow arum, buttonbush, swamp buttercup, and willow provide plant diversity. At 3.4 miles is a patch of wild plum. You will reach a service road (Sunnyvale Drive) at 3.5 miles; turn right. After 80 feet, the red-blazed, 3-mile, pedestrians-only *Deep River Hiking Trail* crosses the road, left and right. (If following *Deep River Hiking Trail* to the right, you will descend on steps, then ascend on bluffs overlooking the creek. You will descend among large yellow poplar, papaw, and hepatica to the scenic, cascading creek at 0.4 mile. Note that as you approach a bridge, an unmarked spur trail to the right ascends 0.2 mile to a grassy area and a horse trail in Gibson Park; if going straight at the four-way crossing of the horse trail, you will arrive at *Twin Pond Trail*. Continue on *Deep River Hiking Trail* across the footbridge. You will pass through pinxter and ironwood, ascend to cross a gas pipeline, and cross the gravel Sunnyvale Drive after another 100 yards. At 0.7 mile, you will reach a junction with *Bicentennial Greenway Trail*, right and left. If going left, it is 0.4 mile to where you started at the junction with *Deep River Hiking Trail*, for a loop of 1.1 miles.

(If, instead of the loop described above, you choose to follow *Deep River Hiking Trail* to the left from *Bicentennial Greenway Trail*, you will descend on steps to a narrow footpath. After 100 feet, you will cross a small stream and enter a low area of willow. You will cross a gas pipeline at 0.4 mile. At 0.5 mile, you will cross a bridge in a cove, then enjoy a display of aster, larkspur, and mint under a power line. High Point City Lake is visible to the left. You will then cross another bridge in a scenic cove and ascend to a junction with *Hollis Rogers Pinewoods Trail* to the right; this 0.4-mile shortcut through a large loblolly pine forest curves around the edge to enter a hardwood forest before descending

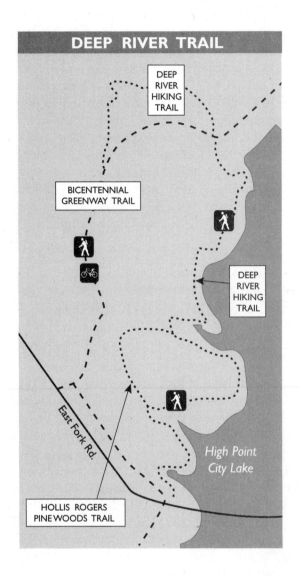

DEEP RIVER TRAIL

DEEP
RIVER
HIKING
TRAIL

BICENTENNIAL
GREENWAY TRAIL

DEEP
RIVER
HIKING
TRAIL

*High Point
City Lake*

East Fork Rd.

HOLLIS ROGERS
PINE WOODS TRAIL

to junction with *Deep River Hiking Trail*. Continuing on *Deep River Hiking Trail*, stay left near the cove and lake through a forest of oak and dogwood to reach the second junction with *Hollis Rogers Pinewoods Trail* at 1.5 miles. You will cross a footbridge, then two more footbridges in coves before arriving at large patches of ground ivy. To the left are views of the lake. You will reach a junction with *Bicentennial Greenway Trail*, right and left, at 2.3 miles.)

If hiking neither of the above-described sections of *Deep River Hiking*

Trail, continue on *Bicentennial Greenway Trail* from its 3.5-mile point. Follow the road for another 150 yards, turn left, and walk steeply uphill. You will cross a pipeline, then cross under a power line, then arrive at Jamestown Park at 4.4 miles. Restrooms and parking facilities are to the right across East Fork Road. Parallel the road; you will reach a junction to the left with *Deep River Hiking Trail* at 4.7 miles. Cross East Fork Road. The next 0.2 mile has a number of boardwalks, bridges, and steps. You will then enter the Piedmont Environmental Center trail network (described above). At 5.8 miles, you will arrive at the parking area of the center. Beyond the center's entrance, the trail descends steeply to High Point City Lake and its south end at Penny Road. Backtrack to the center's parking area. (USGS maps: Guilford, High Point E)

MADISON/MAYODAN

Rockingham County

Madison, like its twin town of Mayodan, has its downtown in the scenic hills between the Dan River on the south and the Mayo River on the east. Named for President James Madison, the town traces its history to 1815; Mayodan was incorporated in 1899. Although in a rural area about halfway between Greensboro and Martinsville, Virginia, the towns are less than isolated. Two major highways—US-311 and US-220—connect here. A charming location to live and work, the towns are also a good place to play. They are near parks such as Hanging Rock State Park to the west, campgrounds such as Beaver Creek to the east, and lakes such as Belews Lake to the south; they also offer 13 miles of freshwater fishing for smallmouth bass, catfish, and sunfish in the Mayo River.

Recently, a 0.25-mile crushed-stone walkway, *Safeway Walking Trail*, was constructed near South Second Street in Mayodan. The popular trail is enjoyed by walkers from a nearby factory, the physically handicapped, and senior citizens. An interpretive marking of trees and a trail extension are planned.

Address: Madison/Mayodan Parks and Recreation Commission, P.O. Box 206 (300 South Second Avenue), Mayodan, NC 27027 (910-548-9572)

Safeway Walking Trail at Madison-Mayodan Recreation Center

Salisbury Station on Salisbury Heritage Trail
Photo courtesy of Rowan County Convention and Visitors Bureau

SALISBURY
Rowan County

This historic city was established in 1755, two years after the colonial governor authorized the creation of Rowan County, which was so large that eventually 26 counties were formed from it. Early settlers streamed into the area from Virginia, Maryland, and Pennsylvania. The town grew into a railroad hub and played a significant role in the Civil War. Before and since that time, Salisbury has been known for commerce, industry, educational institutions, and its Federal, Greek Revival, and Victorian architecture. Part of its heritage is illustrated in the downtown *Salisbury Heritage Tour*, "a walk into history."

The Rowan County Convention and Visitor Bureau offers a map of historic sites; 51 sites are in a 1.3-mile loop and a total of 95 are in a 1.9-

DOWNTOWN SALISBURY

mile loop. Call or write for the map. Briefly, here are some of the high-lights and directions. Start at the Visitor Information Center (Salisbury Station, 1908) on Depot Street and go west one block on East Liberty Street. Turn left (south) on North Lee Street and go two blocks to East Innes Street at 0.2 mile. Turn right (west); halfway down the block is the authentic Rufty's General Store (1905). At the corner is the Kluttz Drug Store Building (1858). Turn left (south) on South Main Street; there is no left turn here for drivers. After one block, turn right (west) on West Fisher Street. Halfway down the block is the Historical Mural (1978–81), which illustrates life at the turn of the 20th century.

Turn left (south) on South Church Street. Halfway down the block on the right side is the Town Well (1760), the city's oldest landmark. Turn right (west) on West Bank Street at 0.5 mile. After crossing South Jack-son Street, you will see the architecturally varied Josephus Hall House

(1820) on the right. At the end of the block, you will reach South Fulton Street. To the left (south) is the longer loop; to the right is the shorter loop. If taking the shorter route, turn right (north) on South Fulton, go one block, then turn right (east) on West Fisher Street. After one block, turn left (north) on Jackson Street. Across the street is Salisbury Female Academy, which dates from 1839. Turn right (east) on West Innes Street, then left (north) on North Church Street, then right (east) on West Council Street. At the east end of the block is the Old Rowan County Courthouse (1855). Turn left (north) on North Main Street. After one block, turn right (east) on East Liberty Street to return to the Visitor Information Center.

Address and Access: Rowan County Convention and Visitor Bureau, P.O. Box 4044, Salisbury, NC (800-332-2343 or 704-638-3100). To reach the Visitor Information Center from I-85, take exit 76, drive west 1 mile on East Innes Street, turn right on Depot Street, and go two blocks.

STATESVILLE
Iredell County

Among Statesville's city parks is the 25-acre Lakewood Park, which contains the 1.6-mile *Lakewood Nature Trail*. To access Lakewood Park from I-40, exit 150, go south 0.4 mile on NC-115 (North Central Street) and turn left on Hartness Road. After 0.3 mile, turn left on Lakewood Drive and proceed to the parking area. From the parking area, follow the trail signs onto a paved and interconnecting trail system in a mature forest of oak, pine, and poplar.

A combination of two beautiful trails is at Mac Anderson Park. To access the park from I-40, exit 150, go 0.3 mile south on NC-115, then turn right on Race Street. Cross Ridgeway Avenue to enter the park, located on the right at 0.6 mile. From the parking lot near the restrooms, begin the paved, 1-mile *Mac Anderson Park Walking Trail* at the signboard. If going north and west through the large hardwoods and pines, you will make a sweeping curve and a gentle descent to a footbridge at 0.7 mile, then reach a junction. (To the right is a dead-end access to a residential area.) The walking trail turns left. Ahead is *Iredell Memorial Trail*, donated by Iredell Memorial Hospital in 1989. On this 1-mile paved

Mac Anderson Park Walking Trail, Statesville

trail, you will gradually ascend a serpentine loop on a grassy knoll. You will pass a fountain and resting benches in areas of locust, oak, and cedar. You will then return to the first trail, cross a footbridge near large tulip poplar, and ascend to the parking area.

Address: Recreation and Parks Department, 440 Signal Hill Drive (P.O. Box 1111), Statesville, NC 28677 (704-878-3429)

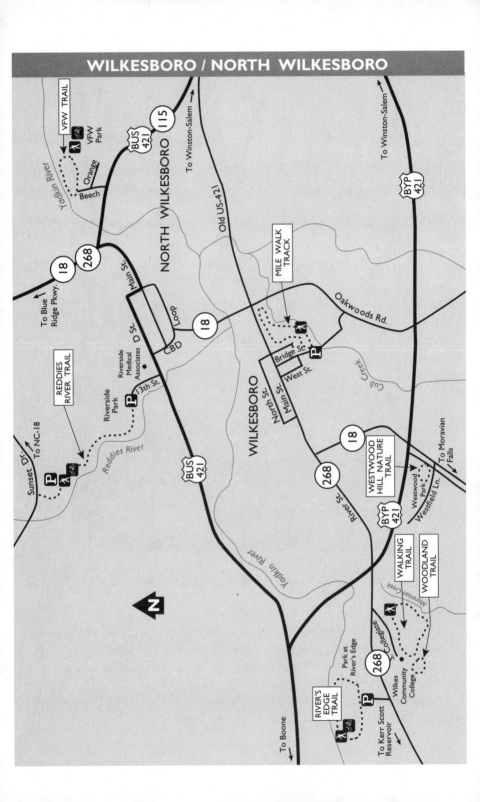

WILKESBORO / NORTH WILKESBORO

WILKESBORO/NORTH WILKESBORO
Wilkes County

Prior to the 18th century, Cherokee Indians had settlements along the Yadkin River, which flows through Wilkes County. By the 1750s, European explorers were in the area. By 1778, Wilkes County was formed. Wilkesboro was incorporated in 1847 and North Wilkesboro in 1891.

The area's hilly terrain identifies it as being in the foothills of the Blue Ridge Mountains; the Blue Ridge Parkway is only 25 miles northwest. South of the towns are the lower-range Brushy Mountains and Moravian Falls.

Wilkesboro and North Wilkesboro offer nine recreational parks, a few of which have walking paths without signs. An example is *VFW Trail* in North Wilkesboro's VFW Park. Suitable for both walking and running, this trail goes behind the park building to the Yadkin River and passes between the baseball field and the tennis courts to form a loop. The facilities at the park include a playground, a concession stand, and restrooms. To access the park from the junction of US-421 Business and NC-18/268, drive 0.3 mile east on US-421 Business, then turn north on Beech Street.

Another walk is on the shady, linear, 1-mile *Reddies River Trail*, which borders the Reddies River. A rocky bank on the east side has rhododendron, mountain laurel, oak, white pine, and wildflowers. This trail was formerly a fitness trail. Access is off US-421 Business; go 0.15 mile on 13th Street and park at Riverside Medical Associates.

In downtown Wilkesboro is a historic walking tour along Cub Creek. The 13 buildings on the *Old Wilkes Walking Tour* are located on Main and North Streets between Woodland Boulevard on the west and Corporation Street on the east. Among the oldest structures is the Old Wilkes Jail, completed in 1860. One of its first inmates was Tom Dooley (or Dula). The restored jail now houses a museum. Another historic site, the Old Law Office, is located across the street from the Tory Oak, which was supposedly used as a hanging tree during the American Revolution. Guided tours can be arranged by calling 919-667-3712, or ask for a brochure at the Wilkes County Courthouse on Main Street.

Wilkesboro's largest, most developed, and most scenic park is Cub Creek Park, which may be accessed by following Bridge Street off Main Street to a parking area near the creek. This park offers picnic shelters,

Reddies River Trail, North Wilkesboro

restrooms, and resting benches beside the water. A 1-mile loop called *Mile Walk Track* passes around five ball fields, two playgrounds, and five tennis courts. The southern half of the trail, near Cub Creek, features large sycamore and river birch. For information about the park, call 910-667-8804.

Another trail is at Westwood Hill Park. To access the park, take Westwood Road off US-421 Bypass for 0.4 mile to West Field, on the right. After ascending 0.1 mile, turn right to the park and the parking lot. Walk around the tennis courts to the west side and descend through white pine on the 0.3-mile loop of *Westwood Hill Nature Trail*. After crossing a footbridge, you will ascend to the point of origin.

There is a short trail at School Street Park, located across the street from Wilkesboro Elementary School. The 0.1-mile *School Street Park Nature Trail* makes a circle on a hillside of pines and hardwoods. To access the park, follow NC-268 west off US-421 Bypass. After 0.1 mile, turn left before crossing the bridge over Moravian Creek and drive 0.6 mile to the school's parking lot.

Wilkes Community College, located in Wilkesboro, has two trails. To access the college, follow NC-268 west off US-421 Bypass. After 0.2 mile, turn left on South Collegiate Street. Drive 0.4 mile and turn left at the campus parking area. From here, you can walk the 1-mile *Walking Trail* clockwise. The trail is wide, smooth, level, and lighted. You will pass a pond, then curve right beside the bank of Moravian Creek at 0.2 mile. There are resting benches along the way. You will leave the creek bank and pass right of a railroad caboose at 0.7 mile. You will then curve right again and pass restrooms and tennis courts to complete the loop.

Near the caboose, you will see a sign about *Woodland Trail*. Follow the street as it ascends slightly toward the Continuing Education Building, but turn up and to the left on the hillside before reaching the parking area. The trail has plant labels. After following switchbacks up the hill, you will reach a ridge and a spur route to the left. Continue on the main trail for a descent to the exit at Whitley Cabin. Turn left to complete the loop after 0.5 mile.

Addresses: Recreation Department, 801 Main Street, North Wilkesboro, NC 28659 (910-838-3359); Parks and Recreation Department, 203 West Main Street, Wilkesboro, NC 28697 (910-838-3951); Wilkes Community College, P.O. Box 120, Wilkesboro, NC 28697 (910-651-8642). For information on other nearby trails, see the sections on W. Kerr Scott Dam and Reservoir in chapter 1, Rendezvous Mountain Educational State Forest in chapter 2, and Wilkes County in chapter 3.

WINSTON-SALEM

Forsyth County

In Winston-Salem, a city/county planning board has established a program that encourages the development of greenway networks for recreation and land-use development. An example is the city's major trail system of *Salem Lake Trail* and *Salem Creek Trail* at Salem Lake,

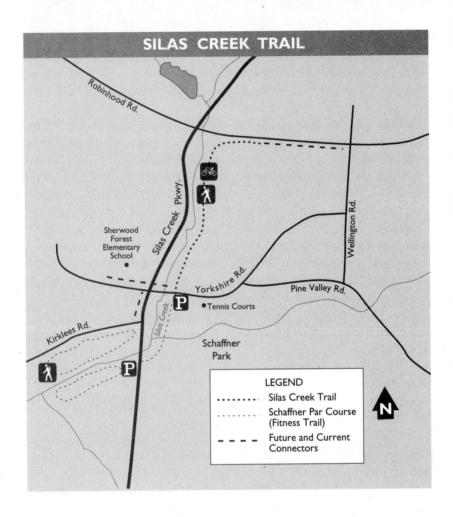

LEGEND

········· Silas Creek Trail

- - - - - - Schaffner Par Course
(Fitness Trail)

– – – Future and Current
Connectors

N

Sherwood
Forest
Elementary
School

Robinhood Rd.

Silas Creek Pkwy.

Wellington Rd.

Yorkshire Rd.

Pine Valley Rd.

Silas Creek

Kirklees Rd.

Tennis Courts

Schaffner
Park

described below. (A loop extension is proposed at the lake's northeast cove of Lowery Creek.)

Other metropolitan trails are at Winston Lake, where an easy, 0.7-mile route runs between the swimming pool parking lot and the picnic shelter. From the swimming pool, it passes through a playground and a gate to enter a mature forest of pine, oak, and poplar near the creek. At 0.3 mile, it passes a physical-fitness station. No camping is allowed. To access the park from I-40 Business, go north on US-311 for 1.9 miles and turn right on Winston Lake Road. Go 0.2 mile to Waterworks Road, turn right, pass the old Winston Lake swimming pool site, go uphill, and turn left to the new YMCA building.

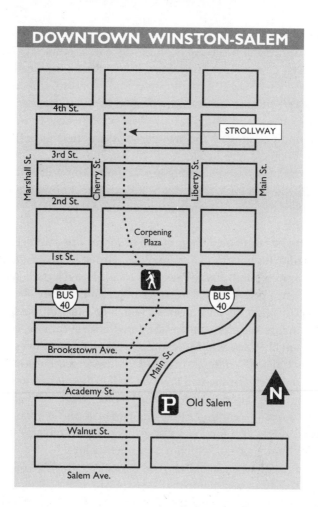

The easy, 0.8-mile *Silas Creek Trail* is a wide greenway from the parking lot at Shaffner Park. To access the trail, turn east off Silas Creek Parkway onto Yorkshire Road and go a few yards to the parking lot, on the right. The trail begins to the left, where it parallels a stream and Silas Creek Parkway. In a mature forest with honeysuckle and wild rose, it crosses a footbridge at 0.4 mile. The northern trailhead does not have a parking lot. Backtrack, or go east for 250 yards on Robinhood Road to a parking lot at a church.

The city's most urban trail is the downtown, 1.2-mile, linear *Strollway Trail*. Street and business parking are available at either end. Access to the southern trailhead is at the corner of Salem Avenue and Liberty

Street, where the trail connects with *Salem Creek Trail* (described below); the northern trailhead is on Fourth Street between Cherry Street and Liberty Street. If starting from the southern trailhead, follow the sign at the west side of Liberty Street and go north. Called the "Super Greenway," this classic metropolitan trail is landscaped with trees, shrubs, flowers, and bridges. Part of its wide treadway is a mixture of asphalt and pea gravel. You will pass Old Salem (right), then pass under I-40 Business at 0.7 mile. You will reach a drinking fountain at 0.9 mile. To the right are glistening skyscrapers. You will reach the northern trailhead at a large archway at Fourth Street downtown. Plans are to extend the trail south from Salem Avenue to the North Carolina School of the Arts.

The city has unnamed short walks at some of its parks. Examples are those at Old Town Park (0.5 mile), Piney Grove Park (0.5 mile), Skyland Park (0.3 mile), and Speas Park (0.4 mile). Longer trails are at Hanes Park, where a popular route runs 1.2 miles on the sidewalk and another 1.2 miles through the park's center, which boasts multiple tennis courts and ball fields and grassy areas scattered with sycamore, oak, and willow; Calvin H. Wiley Middle School towers on the northwest side. Miller Park has trails of 1 mile and 0.5 mile. Little Creek Park has a 0.5-mile walk. A delightful, unnamed 0.2-mile trail is downtown at Spring Park, located near West End Boulevard and Spruce Street north of Sixth Street; the trail descends under a huge oak, passes a picnic table, and crosses two footbridges. Walking can also be enjoyed on physical-fitness trails in 18 city parks, one of which is described below.

For information on 58 of the city's parks, call 910-727-2063 for a *Guide to Parks, Facilities, and Programs*.

Address: Recreation and Parks Department, Box 2511, Winston-Salem, NC 27102 (910-727-2063)

Historic Bethabara Park

Located on Old Town Drive, Historic Bethabara Park has two marked par courses for physical fitness. From the parking area, follow the trail signs and go right in the forest to complete the 0.6-mile southernmost loop on a paved trail. The adjoining paved loop to the north dips into a hollow before returning after 0.4 mile. Virginia pine, dogwood, oak,

Bethabara Trail, Winston-Salem

and tulip poplar are among the dominant trees on the trails.

At the north side of the parking area is a 0.1-mile access to God's Acre, a gated cemetery of Bethabara Moravian Church. A sign at the cemetery states, "No skating, biking, jogging; no pets, food, drinks, or firearms; no boisterous and unseemly conduct; no etching." To the north beyond the cemetery is *God's Acre Nature Trail*, described below.

HISTORIC BETHABARA PARK

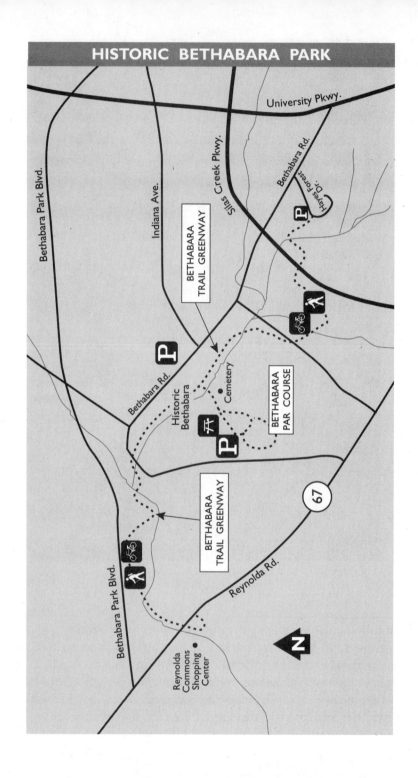

A longer greenway named *Bethabara Trail* and its side trails visit historic sites of the pioneer Moravian settlement. Access is off Silas Creek Parkway. Go west on Bethabara Road past Historic Bethabara Park to a parking lot at the junction with Bonbrook Drive (left); Mill Creek is nearby. To access the southeastern trailhead, turn east off Silas Creek Parkway onto Bethabara Road, then turn right on Hayes Forest Drive (a retirement settlement). Descend to the hollow; the gated trail is on the right, and the only parking lot (intended as residential space) is to the left.

If walking the trail from here, ascend ahead 100 yards to a gate on the right. Descend on *Bethabara Trail*; you will cross a culvert into a mature forest. At 0.4 mile, you will pass through a tunnel under Silas Creek Parkway. You will ascend steps, then follow a narrow foot trail to skirt a residential area. You will descend through a beech grove and ascend steps to Old Town Drive at 0.9 mile. Turn right, go 0.1 mile, and turn left. You will pass through prominent sycamore and poplar at 1.1 miles. To the left at 1.5 miles is *God's Acre Nature Trail*. (This trail ascends steeply for 0.1 mile to the historic hilltop cemetery; backtrack.) To the right are access points to the meadows of Historic Bethabara Park. Continue downstream to Bonbrook Drive at 1.8 miles; the parking lot is to the right.

If continuing across Bonbrook Drive, you will pass a gate. At 2 miles, you will cross an arched metal-and-wooden bridge over Mill Creek. Here, the treadway becomes woodchips for the next 0.4 mile. You will pass under sycamore, elm, tulip poplar, and sweet gum and reach a power line at 2.1 miles. At 2.2 miles, you will cross a creosoted bridge over a small stream. To the left are the remains of a former stone bridge. To the right at 2.3 miles is a marker for Morris Mill (1755), which was located to the left.

You will cross an arched footbridge to a paved greenway (right and left) at 2.4 miles. (To the left, the greenway ends after 120 yards near the corner of Linda Circle and Midkiff Road.) Follow the scenic trail downstream to the right. You will pass under a Reynolda Road (NC-67) bridge. Turn left and exit at the highway at 2.7 miles. Parking is available left across the bridge at Reynolda Commons Shopping Center.

Address and Access: Historic Bethabara Park, 2147 Bethabara Road, Winston-Salem, NC 27106 (910-924-8191). From Reynolda Road at Reynolda Manor Shopping Center, turn north on Old Town Drive and go 0.3 mile to the park entrance, on the right.

Salem Lake Trail, Winston-Salem

Salem Lake Park

This park is a 365-acre city reservoir surrounded by 1,800 acres of land. Activities in the park include picnicking, fishing (for bass, bluegill, catfish, and crappie), boating (rentals are available), horseback riding, biking, birding, and hiking. Water-skiing and swimming are not allowed. The park is open daily except Thursdays; for information, call 910-788-0212.

Access: From I-40 Business, go south on US-311/NC-209 at Claremont Avenue, which becomes Martin Luther King Jr. Drive. After 0.8 mile, turn left on Reynolds Park Road (SR-2740) and go 1.9 miles to Salem Lake Road, on the left.

Salem Lake Trail *(6.9 miles)*
Salem Creek Trail *(4.5 miles)*

Length and Difficulty: 11.4 miles combined, easy to moderate

Trailheads and Description: Park on the right on the approach to the second entrance gate. If hiking *Salem Lake Trail* counterclockwise, begin on the right (northeast) on a wide service road through poplar, oak, beech, Virginia pine, and sweet gum. Ferns, yellow root, sweet pepperbush, sensitive briar, and wild rose grow in the open coves and on the lakeside. At 0.9 mile, you will cross a cement bridge. At 2.7 miles, you will cross a causeway; kingfisher and wild duck frequent the marsh to the right. You will arrive at Linville Road (SR-2662) at 3.4 miles. (To the left, it is 0.7 mile to I-40 Business, exit 10.) Continue on the trail by crossing the causeway to the left and reentering the woods. Follow the service road under a power line at 3.9 miles. You will enjoy a scenic view by the lake at 5 miles.

At 6 miles, you will reach a junction to the left with a causeway and an arched bridge over the lake. (To the right is a gravel service road that leads 0.3 mile to a gate and a parking lot at the end of New Greensboro Road. It goes 1.2 miles east to Linville Road and its junction with I-40 Business, exit 10.) Cross the bridge to a resting bench and a scenic view of the lake. You will walk near the shoreline and descend at the base of the dam at a junction with *Salem Creek Trail* (right) at 6.5 miles. If making a loop, you will cross a low-water bridge and ascend to a gate and

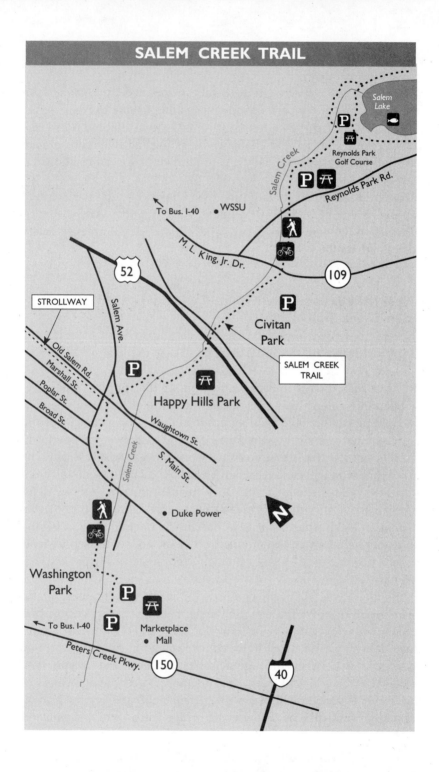

SALEM CREEK TRAIL

Salem Lake

Reynolds Park
Golf Course

Salem Creek

To Bus. I-40   • WSSU

Reynolds Park Rd.

M. L. King, Jr. Dr.

52

109

STROLLWAY

Old Salem Rd.

Marshall St.

Poplar St.

Broad St.

Salem Ave.

Salem Creek

P

Civitan
Park

SALEM CREEK
TRAIL

Happy Hills Park

Waughtown St.

S. Main St.

N

• Duke Power

Washington
Park

To Bus. I-40

P

P

Marketplace
• Mall

Peters Creek Pkwy.

150

40

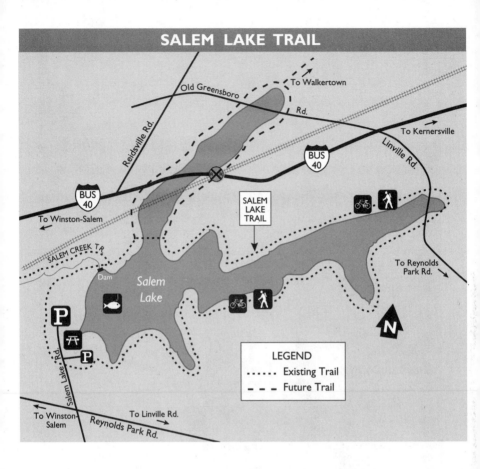

SALEM LAKE TRAIL

LEGEND
...... Existing Trail
– – – Future Trail

the west end of the parking lot; if the gate is locked, follow the paved trail around the fence to the point of origin at 6.9 miles.

Salem Creek Trail parallels Salem Creek downstream through tall poplar, river birch, pine, wild grapevine, and wildflowers. Kudzu is smothering trees and shrubs at a few dense sections. You will pass a picnic table at a cascade at 0.9 mile. You will then pass to the right of Reynolds Park Golf Course and restrooms at 1.4 miles. You will go under Reynolds Park Road, then pass under the Martin Luther King Jr. Drive bridge at 2 miles. To the left is Civitan Park, which has ball fields and a spur footbridge over the creek to the Anderson Center, on the right. The next 0.3 mile offers powerful reminders of urbanization: noise from Vargrave Street and US-52, a high, huge Southern Railroad trestle, and glimpses of the city skyline.

Salem Creek Trail, Winston-Salem

At 3 miles, you will enter the edge of Happy Hills Park, but cross the creek on a footbridge to the wide meadows of the Central Park ball fields. You will then cross Waughtown Street (which goes left to the North Carolina School of the Arts) and junction with *Strollway Trail* (right, described above) at 3.4 miles. Follow the sidewalk past a minimart and turn right off Broad Street into the woods. You will come out of the woods at 3.9 miles and junction with a fitness trail. Ball fields are on both sides of the creek in Washington Park. You will cross an arched footbridge at 4 miles and reach the parking lot at the northwestern corner of Marketplace Mall at 4.5 miles. (It is 0.2 mile farther to Peters Creek Parkway and its junction with Silas Creek Parkway.) Backtrack, or use a second vehicle.

Nat Greene Trail, part of the Mountains-to-Sea Trail,
near Lake Brandt

Chapter 5

MOUNTAINS-TO-SEA TRAIL

Mountains-to-Sea Trail (*MST*), a state trail, passes through the Triad on its way from Clingmans Dome and the *Appalachian Trail* in Great Smoky Mountains National Park to the Nags Head area of the Atlantic coast. Of the proposed foot trail of more than 825 miles, about 375 miles are finished. The completed segments are mainly on federal property in the western part of the state. The *MST* blaze is a white circle with a three-inch diameter.

Nat Greene Trail at Lake Brandt was designated part of the *MST*'s passage through the Triad in 1983. Other sections of the *MST* are planned through Pilot Mountain State Park and Hanging Rock State Park to connect Lake Brandt from the west. East of Lake Brandt, routes are planned into Alamance County to Eno River State Park. Details of the completed routes are included in *North Carolina Hiking Trails*, third edition, by Allen de Hart. Also, the North Carolina Division of Parks and Recreation has prepared a booklet, *An Introduction to North Carolina's* Mountains-to-Sea Trail, for distribution; call 919-846-9991. For the purposes of this guidebook, only an introduction to the history of the *MST* is included.

After the North Carolina General Assembly passed the Trails System Act of 1973, the staff of the Department of Natural Resources and Community Development (DNRCD)—now the Department of Environment, Health, and Natural Resources (DEHNR)—began brainstorming about the future of trails. A catalyst was *Resources for Trails in North Carolina, 1972*, written by staff member Bob Buckner. With fresh ideas about trail purposes and usage, staff planners such as Alan Eaks and Jim Hallsey inspired others to move forward in implementing the Trails System Act. One of the act's statutes explains that "in order to provide for the ever-increasing outdoor recreation needs of an expanded population and in order to promote public access to, travel within, and enjoyment and appreciation of the outdoors, . . . trails should be established in natural scenic areas of the state, and in and near urban areas."

This was also a period when the trend for greenways was on the horizon. Regional councils and county governments were proposing canoe trails and trail connections, and Arch Nichols of the Carolina Mountain Club was proposing a 60-mile hiking trail from Mount Pisgah to Mount Mitchell. Discussing these and many other exciting ideas with the DNRCD staff was the North Carolina Trails Committee, a seven-member citizen advisory board.

The committee began functioning in January 1974 with Louise Chatfield of Greensboro as chair, followed by John Falter of Apex in 1976 and Dr. Doris B. Hammett of Waynesville in 1977. It was Dr. Hammett who led a planning committee for the Fourth National Trails Symposium, held at Lake Junaluska from September 7 to September 10, 1977. Among the distinguished speakers was Howard N. Lee, secretary of DNRCD and former mayor of Chapel Hill. Near the end of his speech, Lee said, "I think the time has come for us to consider the feasibility of establishing a state trail between the mountains and the seashore in North Carolina." He explained that he wanted the Trails Committee to plan a trail that would utilize the National Park Service, the United States Forest Service, state parks, city and county properties, and the property of private landowners "willing to give an easement over a small portion of their land on a legacy to future generations. I don't think we should be locked into the traditional concept of a trail with woods on both sides. . . . I think it would be a trail that would help—like the first primitive trails—bring us together. . . . It would depend on trail enthusiasts for maintenance. . . . Beyond that, how great it would be if other states would follow suit and that the state trails could be linked nationally." After the conference, Curtis Yates of the Department of Transportation sent Lee a map of the *Mountains-to-Sea* bicycle trail, from Murphy to Manteo. Yates inquired if the bike trail could be part of the proposal.

Citizen task forces were established to design, negotiate easements for, construct, and maintain segments of the approximately 20-mile-wide corridor for the "dream trail," whose name became *Mountains-to-Sea Trail*; the *to* was dropped for an easier abbreviation and to avoid the longer *MTST*. Its western trailhead would be at Clingmans Dome as a connector with the *Appalachian Trail* in Great Smoky Mountains National Park and its eastern trailhead at Nags Head on the Outer Banks. Between 1979 and 1981, the DNRCD signed cooperative planning agreements with the National Park Service, the United States Forest Service, and the United States Fish and Wildlife Service for the *MST* to pass

Potential route of Mountains-to-Sea Trail on Lake Brandt Causeway

through federal properties. Another agreement was signed in 1985 pledging a cooperative effort to share resources for the state's longest trail.

According to plans, the *MST* would use original trails in Great Smoky Mountains National Park to reach the Cherokee Indian reservation and the Blue Ridge Parkway. It would follow the Blue Ridge Parkway until reaching Nantahala National Forest, where it would alternate between the properties. It would also alternate between the Blue Ridge Parkway and Pisgah National Forest, with the exception of a long eastern curve into the Davidson River drainage of the Pisgah District and the Linville River and Wilson Creek drainages of the Grandfather District. On its return to the Blue Ridge Parkway at Mount Pisgah, it would follow the parkway's corridor to the Mount Mitchell entrance road before descending to Black Mountain Campground in the Toecane Ranger District of Pisgah National Forest. It would then return to the Blue Ridge Parkway for a short parallel before following Woods Mountain to US-221. From there, the *MST* would stay in the Grandfather District of Pisgah National Forest before returning to the Blue Ridge Parkway at Beacon Heights. It would then follow the parkway to its final eastern turn at the northern edge of Doughton Park.

From there, the *MST* would descend to Stone Mountain State Park, a section to be named in honor of Louise Chatfield (1920–86), a leader in the trails movement and founder of the North Carolina Trails Association in 1978. From Stone Mountain State Park, the *MST* route would enter private or public lands to Pilot Mountain State Park and Hanging Rock State Park. Continuing southeast to Lake Brandt, north of Greensboro, it would pass through Alamance and Durham Counties and approach Eno River State Park in Durham. From there, it would connect with the *Falls Lake Trail* system to Raleigh. From Raleigh, it would follow the floodplains corridor of the Neuse River through Johnston and Wayne Counties to Cliffs-of-the-Neuse State Park and through Lenoir County. It would leave the Neuse River to enter Croatan National Forest in Jones, Pamlico, and Carteret Counties. At Cedar Island, hikers would take a state ferry to Ocracoke, the beginning of the final 75 miles, and follow *Cape Hatteras Beach Trail* on the Outer Banks through Cape Hatteras National Seashore.

In addition to the main *MST* corridor across the state, regional connecting trails could be planned to major cities, Uwharrie National Forest, and other public areas such as state, city, and county parks. A specific route has not been defined. A footpath off the road would require the purchase or lease of nearly 400 miles of private property, the cost of which would make construction unlikely. A less visionary approach has been discussed among trail leaders since the beginning. This plan calls for a multiuse trail to include bike trails, horse trails, rail trails, and back-country roads. In metropolitan areas, sidewalks could be used.

Until a foot trail or a multiuse route is completed from the mountains to the sea, some hikers are choosing to see the state by biking the state's bike network. The longest route, the 700-mile *Mountains-to-Sea Bike Route #2*, is from Murphy to Manteo. It makes a junction with the *MST* foot trail at Balsam Gap at US-23/74 and the Blue Ridge Parkway. *Bike Route #2* follows the Blue Ridge Parkway to NC-181 east of Linville Falls and partway down the mountain, where the two mountains-to-sea trails cross for the last time in the mountains. For 129 miles along the Blue Ridge Parkway, the *MST* plays tag with *Bike Route #2*, crisscrossing the parkway. Bikers are not allowed on the *MST* footpath if on Blue Ridge Parkway property, but hikers may walk the parkway between crossings. Another cross-state route is the 400-mile *North Line Trace Bike Route #4*, which runs close to Stone Mountain State Park, part of the proposed route of the *MST*. This route goes near at least three state parks and a number of county or town parks to Knotts Island. The 170-mile *Ocracoke Option* (Highway F) branches off the *Mountains-to-Sea* bike route west of Wilson at Christian Road (SR-1942) and goes to Cedar Island for the ferry trip to Ocracoke, the general route of the *MST* corridor.

The state's bicycle project began in the Department of Transportation (DOT) in the early 1970s, the same decade that an enthusiastic awareness for statewide foot trails was promoted by the Division of Parks and Recreation. In 1974, Curtis Yates wrote a conceptual paper for a network of biking highways in the state, and Mary Meletiou assisted in the final draft to the state legislature. State Senator McNeill Smith of Greensboro introduced the bill, which easily passed as the North Carolina Bicycle and Bikeway Act of 1974. Both Yates and Meletiou have remained on the DOT staff for more than 20 years as leaders of the network project. Hikers who plan to supplement their passage across the state by biking may request information and maps from the Office of Bicycle and Pedestrian Transportation, Department of Transportation, Box 25201, Raleigh, NC 27611 (919-733-2804). There are 10 routes to choose from, for a total of 3,000 miles.

A few hikers have walked across the state on back roads near the *MST* corridor and short pieces of the state trails system. The first was Lee Price in 1982. Price's feat was sponsored by the North Carolina

Trails Association. He began in Murphy and ended at Cape Hatteras National Seashore. Part of his trek was by bicycle. The most recent through-hike was made by Jeffrey Scott and Jarrett Franklin. They began October 18, 1994, at Nags Head and completed their journey on February 9, 1995, at Clingmans Dome. Of that time, 75 days were continuous backpacking. Graduates of Appalachian State University, they made their hike as part of a project to bring attention to preserving Howard Knob at Boone.

In 1989, the Division of Parks and Recreation's trail staff produced *"Mountains-to-Sea Trail* Proposed Trail Routing and Plan of Action." Its purpose was to incorporate hiking, biking, horseback riding, and canoeing in the passage across the state. The proposal was never fully implemented because priority went to rail trails, greenways, and river trails. Furthermore, the river trails cannot be contiguous. At the June 23 and September 15, 1995, meetings of the North Carolina Trails Committee, the subject was discussed again. The result was a motion by the committee to reaffirm the *MST* concept and encourage the state trails staff to open discussions with the DOT on working together in creating an arrangement of highway bike routes in sections where foot trails have not been completed.

Appendix 1

RESOURCE INFORMATION

The names and addresses listed below of national, state, and Triad organizations associated with trails are intended to supplement those given in the text. For example, most greenway systems allow biking, and some streets and highways have bike routes. The North Carolina Department of Transportation publishes maps of city and county bike routes. An example is the *Winston-Salem/Forsyth County Bike Map*. This detailed map has information on parks, bike shops, and safety; contact the City-County Planning Board of Forsyth County and Winston-Salem, P.O. Box 2511, Winston-Salem, NC 27102 (910-727-2087). Because many hikers and walkers are also bikers, the addresses of a variety of clubs are included here. New residents of the Triad may wish to know about trail clubs or special groups interested in outdoor activities. Some names are included here and others may be available from local chambers of commerce. If users of this guidebook know of organizations not listed, they are encouraged to inform the publisher or the author.

National Organizations

American Birding Association
Box 6599
Colorado Springs, CO 80934
719-634-7736

American Camping Association
5000 State Road, 67N
Martinsville, IN 46151
317-342-8456

American Hiking Society
Box 20160
Washington, DC 20041
703-385-3252

Appalachian Trail Conference
P.O. Box 807
Harpers Ferry, WV 25425
304-535-6331

Boy Scouts of America (national)
Box 152079
Irving, TX 75015
214-580-2000 (Call for information
    on state chapters.)

Friends of the Earth
218 D Street SE
Washington, DC 20003
202-544-2600

Girl Scouts of the USA
420 Fifth Avenue
New York, NY 10018
212-852-8000 (Call for information
    on state chapters.)

National Wildlife Federation
1400 16th Street NW
Washington, DC 20036
202-797-6693

North Carolina
Government Agencies

Department of Commerce, Travel,
    and Tourism
430 North Salisbury Street
Raleigh, NC 27611
919-733-4171

Department of Environment,
    Health, and Natural Resources
    (DEHNR)
Box 27687
Archdale Building, 512 North
    Salisbury Street
Raleigh, NC 27611

919-733-4984
*(Note that the state parks are in
DEHNR but that the address and
telephone number for the park superintendent, the trails director, and
the regional trails specialist are as follows: Yorkshire Center, 12700 Bayleaf
Church Road, Raleigh, NC 27614,
919-846-9991.)*

Department of Transportation
Bicycle Program
Box 25201
Raleigh, NC 27611
919-733-2804

Recreation Resources Service
Box 8004, NCSU
Raleigh, NC 27695
919-515-7118
*(For a fee, this office offers a detailed
directory of municipal, county, college
and university, military, national, and
state parks, forests, and historic sites.
Information on DEHNR offices and a
number of professional organizations
is included.)*

Wildlife Resources Commission
Archdale Building, 512 North
    Salisbury Street
Raleigh, NC 27604
919-733-3391

North Carolina Citizens'
Groups (chiefly in the
Triad area)

Alamance/Burlington Bicycle Club
2569 South Church Street
Burlington, NC 27215
910-226-4116

Audubon Society
P.O. Box 5088
Greensboro, NC 27435

Carolina American Youth Hostels
P.O. Box 10766
Winston-Salem, NC 27108

Dan River Canoe Trail Club
P.O. Box 575
Winston-Salem, NC 27102

Foothills Nature Society
P.O. Box 857
Elkin, NC 28621

Greensboro Fat Tire Society
P.O. Box 9524
Greensboro, NC 27429

Hearts Racing Club
114-J Reynolda Village
Winston-Salem, NC 27106
910-724-1348

High Point Bicycle Club
412 Rockspring Road
High Point, NC 27262

Kernersville Bike Club
101 North Main Street
Kernersville, NC 27284
910-996-4045

North Carolina Horse Council
3535 Freeman Lane
Elon College, NC 27244
910-584-1470

North Carolina Mountain Bike
   Association
5603-D West Friendly Avenue
Greensboro, NC 27410
910-852-3972

North Carolina Off-Road Vehicle
   Association
4501 Temple Hill Church Road
Granite Falls, NC 28630
704-396-7230

North Carolina Rail Trails
703 Ninth Street, Suite 124
Durham, NC 27705
919-493-6394 (Contact this organization for information on other
   chapters.)

Piedmont Appalachian Trail Hikers (PATH)
5113 Woodrun on Tillery
Mount Gilead, NC 27306

Piedmont Flyers Bicycle Club
P.O. Box 5032
Winston-Salem, NC 27106
910-722-2413

Piedmont Hiking and Outdoor
   Club
1400 Knightwood Drive
Greensboro, NC 27410
910-292-7637

Piedmont Horsemans Association
2403 NC-49 South
Asheboro, NC 27203
919-629-9296

Piedmont Land Conservancy
P.O. Box 4025
Greensboro, NC 27404
910-299-2651

Pilot Mountain Trails Committee
P.O. Box 990
Pinnacle, NC 27043

Rockingham Adventure Club
703 Washington Street
Eden, NC 27288
910-635-4793

Sauratown Trail Association
Route 1, Box 527
Pinnacle, NC 27043
910-983-3250

Sierra Club (Foothills Group)
520 West End Boulevard
Winston-Salem, NC 27101
910-723-5198

Sierra Club (Haw River Group)
1529 Brentwood Drive
Graham, NC 27253
910-578-3106

Sierra Club (Piedmont Plateau
   Group)
P.O. Box 5032
Greensboro, NC 27435
910-274-2999

Triad Horsemans Association
P.O. Box 12275
Winston-Salem, NC 27429

Triad Wheelers Bicycle Club
P.O. Box 9812
Greensboro, NC 27429
910-674-0340

Winston Wanderers (Volkswalkers)
P.O. Box 15013
Winston-Salem, NC 27113
910-766-6446

Appendix 2

SPECIAL TRAILS

A few trails in the Triad have been specifically constructed to accommodate the physically handicapped. By the nature of their smooth asphalt paving and low elevation change, some greenways are ideal for wheelchair usage. Examples of these special trails are *Bethabara Trail, Little Walden Trail, Bicentennial Garden Trail, Greensboro Arboretum Trail, Strollway Trail, Silas Creek Trail, Boulding Branch Trail, Salem Creek Trail,* and *Guilford Courthouse Battlefield Trail.*

Families with children have a number of options for nature walks. Some of the educational and interpretive trails are *Densons Creek Nature Trail, Daniel Boone's Cave Trail, Fort Dobbs Nature Trail, Lower Cascades Trail, Upper Cascades Trail, Quarry Trail, Three Rivers Trail, Mountain Loop Trail, Ecology Trail, Sassafras Trail, Rendezvous Mountain Talking Tree Trail, Emerson's Walk, Thoreau's Woods Trail, Lake Trail, Zoo Trail, Greensboro Arboretum Trail, Bicentennial Garden Trail, Bog Garden Trail,* and all the trails at Piedmont Environmental Center.

TRAIL INDEX